Legends & Lyrics: First Series by Adelaide Anne Procter

Adelaide Anne Procter was born at 25 Bedford Square in Bloomsbury, on October 30th, 1825. An early voracious reader she began her literary career as a teenager; her poems were primarily published in Charles Dickens's periodicals Household Words and All the Year Round and later published in book form.

Her charity work and her conversion to Roman Catholicism in 1851 seems to have been a strong influence on her poetry and her desire to help the homeless and unemployed women as well as work with feminist groups and various journals. Adelaide was a favourite poet of Queen Victoria and fellow poet Coventry Patmore called her "the most popular poet of the day after Alfred Lord Tennyson". Many of her poems were set to music and published in England, Germany and the United States.

Adelaide never married and this has given rise to questions about her sexuality. Her poems do reveal how Victorian women expressed repressed feelings but for many years now her work has to been given the attention it really deserves. Here we publish volume 1 of her poems so her work can now be seen for the great talent that she is.

Adelaide Anne Proctor died on February 2nd 1864 from tuberculosis at the age of only 38.

Index of Contents

DEDICATION

TO MATILDA M. HAYS.

"Our tokens of love are for the most part barbarous. Cold and lifeless, because they do not represent our life. The only gift is a portion of thyself. Therefore let the farmer give his corn; the miner, a gem; the sailor, coral and shells; the painter, his picture; and the poet, his poem." Emerson's Essays.

A. A. P.
May, 1858

AN INTRODUCTION BY CHARLES DICKENS

In the spring of the year 1853, I observed, as conductor of the weekly journal Household Words, a short poem among the proffered contributions, very different, as I thought, from the shoal of verses perpetually setting through the office of such a periodical, and possessing much more merit. Its authoress was quite unknown to me. She was one Miss Mary Berwick, whom I had never heard of; and she was to be addressed by letter, if addressed at all, at a circulating library in the western district of London. Through this channel, Miss Berwick was informed that her poem was accepted, and was invited to send another. She complied, and became a regular and frequent contributor. Many letters passed between the journal and Miss Berwick, but Miss Berwick herself was never seen.

How we came gradually to establish, at the office of Household Words, that we knew all about Miss Berwick, I have never discovered. But we settled somehow, to our complete satisfaction, that she was governess in a family; that she went to Italy in that capacity, and returned; and that she had long been in the same family. We really knew nothing whatever of her, except that she was remarkably business-like, punctual, self-reliant, and reliable: so I suppose we insensibly invented the rest. For myself, my mother was not a more real personage to me, than Miss Berwick the governess became.

This went on until December, 1854, when the Christmas number, entitled The Seven Poor Travellers, was sent to press. Happening to be going to dine that day with an old and dear friend, distinguished in literature as Barry Cornwall, I took with me an early proof of that number, and remarked, as I laid it on the drawing-room table, that it contained a very pretty poem, written by a certain Miss Berwick. Next day brought me the disclosure that I had so spoken of the poem to the mother of its writer, in its writer's presence; that I had no such correspondent in existence as Miss Berwick; and that the name had been assumed by Barry Cornwall's eldest daughter, Miss Adelaide Anne Procter.

The anecdote I have here noted down, besides serving to explain why the parents of the late Miss Procter have looked to me for these poor words of remembrance of their lamented child, strikingly illustrates the honesty, independence, and quiet dignity, of the lady's character. I had known her when she was very young; I had been honoured with her father's friendship when I was myself a young aspirant; and she had said at home, "If I send him, in my own name, verses that he does not honestly like, either it will be very painful to him to return them, or he will print them for papa's sake, and not for their own. So I have made up my mind to take my chance fairly with the unknown volunteers."

Perhaps it requires an editor's experience of the profoundly unreasonable grounds on which he is often urged to accept unsuitable articles, such as having been to school with the writer's husband's brother-in-law, or having lent an alpenstock in Switzerland to the writer's wife's nephew, when that interesting stranger had broken his own, fully to appreciate the delicacy and the self-respect of this resolution.

Some verses by Miss Procter had been published in the Book of Beauty, ten years before she became Miss Berwick. With the exception of two poems in the Cornhill Magazine, two in Good Words, and others in a little book called A Chaplet of Verses (issued in 1862 for the benefit of a Night Refuge), her published writings first appeared in Household Words, or All the Year Round. The present edition contains the whole of her Legends and Lyrics, and originates in the great favour with which they have been received by the public.

Miss Procter was born in Bedford Square, London, on the 30th of October, 1825. Her love of poetry was conspicuous at so early an age, that I have before me a tiny album made of small note-paper, into which her favourite passages were copied for her by her mother's hand before she herself could write. It looks as if she had carried it about, as another little girl might have carried a doll. She soon displayed a remarkable memory, and great quickness of apprehension. When she was quite a young child, she learned with facility several of the problems of Euclid. As she grew older, she acquired the French, Italian, and German languages; became a clever pianoforte player; and showed a true taste and sentiment in drawing. But, as soon as she had completely vanquished the difficulties of any one branch of study, it was her way to lose interest in it, and pass to another. While her mental resources were being trained, it was not at all suspected in her family that she had any gift of authorship, or any ambition to become a writer. Her father had no idea of her having ever attempted to turn a rhyme, until her first little poem saw the light in print.

When she attained to womanhood, she had read an extraordinary number of books, and throughout her life she was always largely adding to the number. In 1853 she went to Turin and its neighbourhood, on a visit to her aunt, a Roman Catholic lady. As Miss Procter had herself professed the Roman Catholic Faith two years before, she entered with the greater ardour on the study of the Piedmontese dialect, and the observation of the habits and manners of the peasantry. In the former, she soon became a proficient. On the latter head, I extract from her familiar letters written home to England at the time, two pleasant pieces of description.

A BETROTHAL

"We have been to a ball, of which I must give you a description. Last Tuesday we had just done dinner at about seven, and stepped out into the balcony to look at the remains of the sunset behind the mountains, when we heard very distinctly a band of music, which rather excited my astonishment, as a solitary organ is the utmost that toils up here. I went out of the room for a few minutes, and, on my returning, Emily said, 'Oh! That band is playing at the farmer's near here. The daughter is fiancee to-day, and they have a ball.' I said, 'I wish I was going!' 'Well,' replied she, 'the farmer's wife did call to invite us.' 'Then I shall certainly go,' I exclaimed. I applied to Madame B., who said she would like it very much, and we had better go, children and all. Some of the servants were already gone. We rushed away to put on some shawls, and put off any shred of black we might have about us (as the people would have been quite annoyed if we had appeared on such an occasion with any black), and we started. When we reached the farmer's, which is a stone's throw above our house, we were received with great enthusiasm; the only drawback being, that no one spoke French, and we did not yet speak Piedmontese. We were placed on a bench against the wall, and the people went on dancing. The room was a large whitewashed kitchen (I suppose), with several large pictures in black frames, and very smoky. I distinguished the Martyrdom of Saint Sebastian, and the others appeared equally lively and appropriate subjects. Whether they were Old Masters or not, and if so, by whom, I could not ascertain. The band were seated opposite us. Five men, with wind instruments, part of the band of the National Guard, to which the farmer's sons belong. They played really admirably, and I began to be afraid that some idea of our dignity would prevent me getting a partner; so, by Madame B.'s advice, I went up to the bride, and offered to dance with her. Such a handsome young woman! Like one of Uwins's pictures. Very dark, with a quantity of black hair, and on an immense scale. The children were already dancing, as well as the maids. After we came to an end of our dance, which was what they called a Polka-Mazourka, I saw the bride trying to screw up the courage of her fiance to ask me to dance, which after a little hesitation he did. And admirably he danced, as indeed they all did, in excellent time, and with a little more spirit than one sees in a ball-room. In fact, they were very like one's ordinary partners, except that they wore earrings and were in their shirt-sleeves, and truth compels me to state that they decidedly smelt of garlic. Some of them had been smoking, but threw away their cigars when we came in. The only thing that did not look cheerful was, that the room was only lighted by two or three oil-lamps, and that there seemed to be no preparation for refreshments. Madame B., seeing this, whispered to her maid, who disengaged herself from her partner, and ran off to the house; she and the kitchenmaid presently returning with a large tray covered with all kinds of cakes (of which we are great consumers and always have a stock), and a large hamper full of bottles of wine, with coffee and sugar. This seemed all very acceptable. The fiancee was requested to distribute the eatables, and a bucket of water being produced to wash the glasses in, the wine disappeared very quickly, as fast as they could open the bottles. But, elated, I suppose, by this, the floor was sprinkled with water, and the musicians played a Monferrino, which is a Piedmontese dance. Madame B. danced with the farmer's son, and Emily with another distinguished member of the company. It was very fatiguing, something like a Scotch reel. My partner was a little man, like Perrot, and very proud of his dancing. He cut in the air and twisted about, until I was out of breath, though my attempts to imitate him were feeble in the extreme. At last, after seven or eight dances, I was obliged to sit down. We stayed till nine, and I was so dead beat with the heat that I could hardly crawl about the house, and in an agony with the cramp, it is so long since I have danced."

A MARRIAGE

The wedding of the farmer's daughter has taken place. We had hoped it would have been in the little chapel of our house, but it seems some special permission was necessary, and they applied for it too late. They all said, "This is the Constitution. There would have been no difficulty before!" the lower classes making the poor Constitution the scapegoat for everything they don't like. So as it was impossible for us to climb up to the church where the wedding was to be, we contented ourselves with seeing the procession pass. It was not a very large one, for, it requiring some activity to go up, all the old people remained at home. It is not etiquette for the bride's mother to go, and no unmarried woman can go to a wedding, I suppose for fear of its making her discontented with her own position. The procession stopped at our door, for the bride to receive our congratulations. She was dressed in a shot silk, with a yellow handkerchief, and rows of a large gold chain. In the afternoon they sent to request us to go there. On our arrival we found them dancing out of doors, and a most melancholy affair it was. All the bride's sisters were not to be recognised, they had cried so. The mother sat in the house, and could not appear. And the bride was sobbing so, she could hardly stand! The most melancholy spectacle of all to my mind was, that the bridegroom was decidedly tipsy. He seemed rather affronted at all the distress. We danced a Monferrino; I with the bridegroom; and the bride crying the whole time. The company did their utmost to enliven her by firing pistols, but without success, and at last they began a series of yells, which reminded me of a set of savages. But even this delicate method of consolation failed, and the wishing good-bye began. It was altogether so melancholy an affair that Madame B. dropped a few tears, and I was very near it, particularly when the poor mother came out to see the last of her daughter, who was finally dragged off between her brother and uncle, with a last explosion of pistols. As she lives quite near, makes an excellent match, and is one of nine children, it really was a most desirable marriage, in spite of all the show of distress. Albert was so discomfited by it, that he forgot to kiss the bride as he had intended to do, and therefore went to call upon her yesterday, and found her very smiling in her new house, and supplied the omission. The cook came home from the wedding, declaring she was cured of any wish to marry, but I would not recommend any man to act upon that threat and make her an offer. In a couple of days we had some rolls of the bride's first baking, which they call Madonnas. The musicians, it seems, were in the same state as the bridegroom, for, in escorting her home, they all fell down in the mud. My wrath against the bridegroom is somewhat calmed by finding that it is considered bad luck if he does not get tipsy at his wedding."

Those readers of Miss Procter's poems who should suppose from their tone that her mind was of a gloomy or despondent cast, would be curiously mistaken. She was exceedingly humorous, and had a great delight in humour. Cheerfulness was habitual with her, she was very ready at a sally or a reply, and in her laugh (as I remember well) there was an unusual vivacity, enjoyment, and sense of drollery. She was perfectly unconstrained and unaffected: as modestly silent about her productions, as she was generous with their pecuniary results. She was a friend who inspired the strongest attachments; she was a finely sympathetic woman, with a great accordant heart and a sterling noble nature. No claim can be set up for her, thank God, to the possession of any of the conventional poetical qualities. She never by any means held the opinion that she was among the greatest of human beings; she never suspected the existence of a conspiracy on the part of mankind against her; she never recognised in her best friends, her worst enemies; she never cultivated the luxury of being misunderstood and unappreciated; she would far rather have died without seeing a line of her composition in print, than that I should have maundered about her, here, as "the Poet", or "the Poetess".

With the recollection of Miss Procter as a mere child and as a woman, fresh upon me, it is natural that I should linger on my way to the close of this brief record, avoiding its end. But, even as the close came upon her, so must it come here.

Always impelled by an intense conviction that her life must not be dreamed away, and that her indulgence in her favourite pursuits must be balanced by action in the real world around her, she was indefatigable in her endeavours to do some good. Naturally enthusiastic, and conscientiously impressed with a deep sense of her Christian duty to her neighbour, she devoted herself to a variety of benevolent objects. Now, it was the visitation of the sick, that had possession of her; now, it was the sheltering of the houseless; now, it was the elementary teaching of the densely ignorant; now, it was the raising up of those who had wandered and got trodden under foot; now, it was the wider employment of her own sex in the general business of life; now, it was all these things at once. Perfectly unselfish, swift to sympathise and eager to relieve, she wrought at such designs with a flushed earnestness that disregarded season, weather, time of day or night, food, rest. Under such a hurry of the spirits, and such incessant occupation, the strongest constitution will commonly go down. Hers, neither of the strongest nor the weakest, yielded to the burden, and began to sink.

To have saved her life, then, by taking action on the warning that shone in her eyes and sounded in her voice, would have been impossible, without changing her nature. As long as the power of moving about in the old way was left to her, she must exercise it, or be killed by the restraint. And so the time came when she could move about no longer, and took to her bed.

All the restlessness gone then, and all the sweet patience of her natural disposition purified by the resignation of her soul, she lay upon her bed through the whole round of changes of the seasons. She lay upon her bed through fifteen months. In all that time, her old cheerfulness never quitted her. In all that time, not an impatient or a querulous minute can be remembered.

At length, at midnight on the second of February, 1864, she turned down a leaf of a little book she was reading, and shut it up.

The ministering hand that had copied the verses into the tiny album was soon around her neck, and she quietly asked, as the clock was on the stroke of one:

"Do you think I am dying, mamma?"

"I think you are very, very ill to-night, my dear!"

"Send for my sister. My feet are so cold. Lift me up?"

Her sister entering as they raised her, she said: "It has come at last!"

And with a bright and happy smile, looked upward, and departed.

Well had she written:

Why shouldst thou fear the beautiful angel, Death,
Who waits thee at the portals of the skies,
Ready to kiss away thy struggling breath,
Ready with gentle hand to close thine eyes?

Oh what were life, if life were all? Thine eyes
Are blinded by their tears, or thou wouldst see
Thy treasures wait thee in the far-off skies,
And Death, thy friend, will give them all to thee.

LEGENDS & LYRICS: FIRST SERIES

THE ANGEL'S STORY

Through the blue and frosty heavens
Christmas stars were shining bright;
Glistening lamps throughout the City
Almost matched their gleaming light;
While the winter snow was lying,
And the winter winds were sighing,
Long ago, one Christmas night.

While, from every tower and steeple,
Pealing bells were sounding clear,
(Never with such tones of gladness,
Save when Christmas time is near,)
Many a one that night was merry
Who had toiled through all the year.

That night saw old wrongs forgiven,
Friends, long parted, reconciled;
Voices all unused to laughter,
Mournful eyes that rarely smiled,
Trembling hearts that feared the morrow,
From their anxious thoughts beguiled.

Rich and poor felt love and blessing
From the gracious season fall;
Joy and plenty in the cottage,
Peace and feasting in the hall;
And the voices of the children
Ringing clear above it all!

Yet one house was dim and darkened;
Gloom, and sickness, and despair,
Dwelling in the gilded chambers.
Creeping up the marble stair,
Even stilled the voice of mourning
For a child lay dying there.

Silken curtains fell around him,
Velvet carpets hushed the tread.
Many costly toys were lying,
All unheeded, by his bed;
And his tangled golden ringlets
Were on downy pillows spread.

The skill of all that mighty City
To save one little life was vain;
One little thread from being broken,
One fatal word from being spoken;
Nay, his very mother's pain,
And the mighty love within her,
Could not give him health again.

So she knelt there still beside him,
She alone with strength to smile,
Promising that he should suffer
No more in a little while,
Murmuring tender song and story
Weary hours to beguile.

Suddenly an unseen Presence
Checked those constant moaning cries,
Stilled the little heart's quick fluttering,
Raised those blue and wondering eyes,
Fixed on some mysterious vision,
With a startled sweet surprise.

For a radiant angel hovered,
Smiling, o'er the little bed;
White his raiment, from his shoulders
Snowy dove-like pinions spread,
And a starlike light was shining
In a Glory round his head.

While, with tender love, the angel,
Leaning o'er the little nest,
In his arms the sick child folding,
Laid him gently on his breast,
Sobs and wailings told the mother
That her darling was at rest.

So the angel, slowing rising,
Spread his wings; and, through the air,
Bore the child, and while he held him
To his heart with loving care,
Placed a branch of crimson roses
Tenderly beside him there.

While the child, thus clinging, floated
Towards the mansions of the Blest,
Gazing from his shining guardian
To the flowers upon his breast,
Thus the angel spake, still smiling
On the little heavenly guest:

"Know, dear little one, that Heaven
Does no earthly thing disdain,
Man's poor joys find there an echo
Just as surely as his pain;
Love, on earth so feebly striving,
Lives divine in Heaven again!

"Once in that great town below us,
In a poor and narrow street,

Dwelt a little sickly orphan;
Gentle aid, or pity sweet,
Never in life's rugged pathway
Guided his poor tottering feet.

"All the striving anxious forethought
That should only come with age,
Weighed upon his baby spirit,
Showed him soon life's sternest page;
Grim Want was his nurse, and Sorrow
Was his only heritage.

"All too weak for childish pastimes,
Drearily the hours sped;
On his hands so small and trembling
Leaning his poor aching head,
Or, through dark and painful hours,
Lying sleepless on his bed.

"Dreaming strange and longing fancies
Of cool forests far away;
And of rosy, happy children,
Laughing merrily at play,
Coming home through green lanes, bearing
Trailing boughs of blooming May.

"Scarce a glimpse of azure heaven
Gleamed above that narrow street,
And the sultry air of Summer
(That you call so warm and sweet)
Fevered the poor Orphan, dwelling
In the crowded alley's heat.

"One bright day, with feeble footsteps
Slowly forth he tried to crawl,
Through the crowded city's pathways,
Till he reached a garden-wall;
Where 'mid princely halls and mansions
Stood the lordliest of all.

"There were trees with giant branches,
Velvet glades where shadows hide;
There were sparkling fountains glancing,
Flowers, which in luxuriant pride
Even wafted breaths of perfume
To the child who stood outside.

"He against the gate of iron
Pressed his wan and wistful face,
Gazing with an awe-struck pleasure
At the glories of the place;

Never had his brightest day-dream
Shone with half such wondrous grace.

"You were playing in that garden,
Throwing blossoms in the air,
Laughing when the petals floated
Downwards on your golden hair;
And the fond eyes watching o'er you,
And the splendour spread before you,
Told a House's Hope was there.

"When your servants, tired of seeing
Such a face of want and woe,
Turning to the ragged Orphan,
Gave him coin, and bade him go,
Down his cheeks so thin and wasted,
Bitter tears began to flow.

"But that look of childish sorrow
On your tender child-heart fell,
And you plucked the reddest roses
From the tree you loved so well,
Passed them through the stern cold grating,
Gently bidding him 'Farewell!'

"Dazzled by the fragrant treasure
And the gentle voice he heard,
In the poor forlorn boy's spirit,
Joy, the sleeping Seraph, stirred;
In his hand he took the flowers,
In his heart the loving word.

"So he crept to his poor garret;
Poor no more, but rich and bright,
For the holy dreams of childhood
Love, and Rest, and Hope, and Light
Floated round the Orphan's pillow
Through the starry summer night.

"Day dawned, yet the visions lasted;
All too weak to rise he lay;
Did he dream that none spake harshly
All were strangely kind that day?
Surely then his treasured roses
Must have charmed all ills away.

"And he smiled, though they were fading;
One by one their leaves were shed;
'Such bright things could never perish,
They would bloom again,' he said.
When the next day's sun had risen

Child and flowers both were dead.

"Know, dear little one! our Father
Will no gentle deed disdain;
Love on the cold earth beginning
Lives divine in Heaven again,
While the angel hearts that beat there
Still all tender thoughts retain."

So the angel ceased, and gently
O'er his little burthen leant;
While the child gazed from the shining,
Loving eyes that o'er him bent,
To the blooming roses by him,
Wondering what that mystery meant.

Thus the radiant angel answered,
And with tender meaning smiled:
"Ere your childlike, loving spirit,
Sin and the hard world defiled,
God has given me leave to seek you
I was once that little child!"

In the churchyard of that city
Rose a tomb of marble rare,
Decked, as soon as Spring awakened,
With her buds and blossoms fair
And a humble grave beside it
No one knew who rested there.

ECHOES

Still the angel stars are shining,
Still the rippling waters flow,
But the angel-voice is silent
That I heard so long ago.
Hark! the echoes murmur low,
Long ago!

Still the wood is dim and lonely,
Still the plashing fountains play,
But the past and all its beauty,
Whither has it fled away?
Hark! the mournful echoes say,
Fled away!

Still the bird of night complaineth,
(Now, indeed, her song is pain,)
Visions of my happy hours,

Do I call and call in vain?
Hark! the echoes cry again,
All in vain!

Cease, oh echoes, mournful echoes!
Once I loved your voices well;
Now my heart is sick and weary
Days of old, a long farewell!
Hark! the echoes sad and dreary
Cry farewell, farewell!

A FALSE GENIUS

I see a Spirit by thy side,
Purple-winged and eagle-eyed,
Looking like a Heavenly guide.

Though he seem so bright and fair,
Ere thou trust his proffered care,
Pause a little, and beware!

If he bid thee dwell apart,
Tending some ideal smart
In a sick and coward heart;

In self-worship wrapped alone,
Dreaming thy poor griefs are grown
More than other men have known;

Dwelling in some cloudy sphere,
Though God's work is waiting here,
And God deigneth to be near;

If his torch's crimson glare
Show thee evil everywhere,
Tainting all the wholesome air;

While with strange distorted choice,
Still disdaining to rejoice,
Thou wilt hear a wailing voice;

If a simple, humble heart,
Seem to thee a meaner part,
Than thy noblest aim and art;

If he bid thee bow before
Crowned Mind and nothing more,
The great idol men adore;

And with starry veil enfold
Sin, the trailing serpent old,
Till his scales shine out like gold;

Though his words seem true and wise,
Soul, I say to thee Arise.
He is a Demon in disguise!

MY PICTURE

Stand this way, more near the window
By my desk, you see the light
Falling on my picture better
Thus I see it while I write!

Who the head may be I know not,
But it has a student air;
With a look half sad, half stately,
Grave sweet eyes and flowing hair.

Little care I who the painter,
How obscure a name he bore;
Nor, when some have named Velasquez,
Did I value it the more.

As it is, I would not give it
For the rarest piece of art;
It has dwelt with me, and listened
To the secrets of my heart.

Many a time, when to my garret,
Weary, I returned at night,
It has seemed to look a welcome
That has made my poor room bright.

Many a time, when ill and sleepless,
I have watched the quivering gleam
Of my lamp upon that picture,
Till it faded in my dream.

When dark days have come, and friendship
Worthless seemed, and life in vain,
That bright friendly smile has sent me
Boldly to my task again.

Sometimes when hard need has pressed me
To bow down where I despise,
I have read stern words of counsel
In those sad reproachful eyes.

Nothing that my brain imagined,
Or my weary hand has wrought,
But it watched the dim Idea
Spring forth into armed Thought.

It has smiled on my successes,
Raised me when my hopes were low,
And by turns has looked upon me
With all the loving eyes I know.

Do you wonder that my picture
Has become so like a friend?
It has seen my life's beginnings,
It shall stay and cheer the end!

JUDGE NOT

Judge not; the workings of his brain
And of his heart thou canst not see;
What looks to thy dim eyes a stain,
In God's pure light may only be
A scar, brought from some well-won field,
Where thou wouldst only faint and yield.

The look, the air, that frets thy sight,
May be a token, that below
The soul has closed in deadly fight
With some infernal fiery foe,
Whose glance would scorch thy smiling grace,
And cast thee shuddering on thy face!

The fall thou darest to despise
May be the angel's slackened hand
Has suffered it, that he may rise
And take a firmer, surer stand;
Or, trusting less to earthly things,
May henceforth learn to use his wings.

And judge none lost; but wait, and see,
With hopeful pity, not disdain;
The depth of the abyss may be
The measure of the height of pain
And love and glory that may raise
This soul to God in after days!

FRIEND SORROW

Do not cheat thy Heart and tell her,
"Grief will pass away,
Hope for fairer times in future,
And forget to-day."
Tell her, if you will, that sorrow
Need not come in vain;
Tell her that the lesson taught her
Far outweighs the pain.

Cheat her not with the old comfort,
"Soon she will forget"
Bitter truth, alas but matter
Rather for regret;
Bid her not "Seek other pleasures,
Turn to other things:"
Rather nurse her caged sorrow
'Till the captive sings.

Rather bid her go forth bravely.
And the stranger greet;
Not as foe, with spear and buckler,
But as dear friends meet;
Bid her with a strong clasp hold her,
By her dusky wings
Listening for the murmured blessing
Sorrow always brings.

ONE BY ONE

One by one the sands are flowing,
One by one the moments fall;
Some are coming, some are going;
Do not strive to grasp them all.

One by one thy duties wait thee,
Let thy whole strength go to each,
Let no future dreams elate thee,
Learn thou first what these can teach.

One by one (bright gifts from Heaven)
Joys are sent thee here below;
Take them readily when given,
Ready too to let them go.

One by one thy griefs shall meet thee,
Do not fear an armed band;
One will fade as others greet thee;
Shadows passing through the land.

Do not look at life's long sorrow;
See how small each moment's pain;
God will help thee for to-morrow,
So each day begin again.

Every hour that fleets so slowly
Has its task to do or bear;
Luminous the crown, and holy,
When each gem is set with care.

Do not linger with regretting,
Or for passing hours despond;
Nor, the daily toil forgetting,
Look too eagerly beyond.

Hours are golden links, God's token,
Reaching Heaven; but one by one
Take them, lest the chain be broken
Ere the pilgrimage be done.

TRUE HONOURS

Is my darling tired already,
Tired of her day of play?
Draw your little stool beside me,
Smooth this tangled hair away.
Can she put the logs together,
Till they make a cheerful blaze?
Shall her blind old Uncle tell her
Something of his youthful days?

Hark! The wind among the cedars
Waves their white arms to and fro;
I remember how I watched them
Sixty Christmas Days ago:
Then I dreamt a glorious vision
Of great deeds to crown each year
Sixty Christmas Days have found me
Useless, helpless, blind and here!

Yes, I feel my darling stealing
Warm soft fingers into mine
Shall I tell her what I fancied
In that strange old dream of mine?
I was kneeling by the window,
Reading how a noble band,
With the red cross on their breast-plates,
Went to gain the Holy Land.

While with eager eyes of wonder
Over the dark page I bent,
Slowly twilight shadows gathered
Till the letters came and went;
Slowly, till the night was round me;
Then my heart beat loud and fast,
For I felt before I saw it
That a spirit near me passed.

Then I raised my eyes, and shining
Where the moon's first ray was bright
Stood a winged Angel-warrior
Clothed and panoplied in light:
So, with Heaven's love upon him,
Stern in calm and resolute will,
Looked St. Michael, does the picture
Hang in the old cloister still?

Threefold were the dreams of honour
That absorbed my heart and brain;
Threefold crowns the Angel promised,
Each one to be bought by pain:
While he spoke, a threefold blessing
Fell upon my soul like rain.
HELPER OF THE POOR AND SUFFERING;
VICTOR IN A GLORIOUS STRIFE;
SINGER OF A NOBLE POEM:
Such the honours of my life.

Ah, that dream! Long years that gave me
Joy and grief as real things
Never touched the tender memory
Sweet and solemn that it brings
Never quite effaced the feeling
Of those white and shadowing wings.

Do those blue eyes open wider?
Does my faith too foolish seem?
Yes, my darling, years have taught me
It was nothing but a dream.
Soon, too soon, the bitter knowledge
Of a fearful trial rose,
Rose to crush my heart, and sternly
Bade my young ambition close.

More and more my eyes were clouded,
Till at last God's glorious light
Passed away from me forever,
And I lived and live in night.
Dear, I will not dim your pleasure,

Christmas should be only gay
In my night the stars have risen,
And I wait the dawn of day.

Spite of all I could be happy;
For my brothers' tender care
In their boyish pastimes ever
Made me take, or feel a share.
Philip, even then so thoughtful,
Max so noble, brave and tall,
And your father, little Godfrey,
The most loving of them all.

Philip reasoned down my sorrow,
Max would laugh my gloom away,
Godfrey's little arms put round me,
Helped me through my dreariest day;
While the promise of my Angel,
Like a star, now bright, now pale,
Hung in blackest night above me,
And I felt it could not fail.

Years passed on, my brothers left me,
Each went out to take his share
In the struggle of life; my portion
Was a humble one to bear.
Here I dwelt, and learnt to wander
Through the woods and fields alone,
Every cottage in the village
Had a corner called my own.

Old and young, all brought their troubles,
Great or small, for me to hear;
I have often blessed my sorrow
That drew others' grief so near.
Ah, the people needed helping
Needed love (for Love and Heaven
Are the only gifts not bartered,
They alone are freely given)

And I gave it. Philip's bounty,
(We were orphans, dear,) made toil
Prosper, and want never fastened
On the tenants of the soil.
Philip's name (Oh, how I gloried,
He so young, to see it rise!)
Soon grew noted among statesmen
As a patriot true and wise.

And his people all felt honoured
To be ruled by such a name;

I was proud too that they loved me;
Through their pride in him it came.
He had gained what I had longed for,
I meanwhile grew glad and gay,
'Mid his people, to be serving
Him and them, in some poor way.

How his noble earnest speeches,
With untiring fervour came;
HELPER OF THE POOR AND SUFFERING;
Truly he deserved the name!
Had my Angel's promise failed me?
Had that word of hope grown dim?
Why, my Philip had fulfilled it,
And I loved it best in him!

Max meanwhile ah, you, my darling,
Can his loving words recall
'Mid the bravest and the noblest,
Braver, nobler, than them all.
How I loved him! how my heart thrilled
When his sword clanked by his side.
When I touched his gold embroidery,
Almost saw him in his pride!

So we parted; he all eager
To uphold the name he bore,
Leaving in my charge, he loved me
Someone whom he loved still more:
I must tend this gentle flower,
I must speak to her of him,
For he feared. Love still is fearful
That his memory might grow dim.

I must guard her from all sorrow,
I must play a brother's part,
Shield all grief and trial from her,
If it need be, with my heart.
Years passed, and his name grew famous;
We were proud, both she and I;
And we lived upon his letters,
While the slow days fleeted by.

Then at last, you know the story,
How a fearful rumour spread,
Till all hope had slowly faded,
And we heard that he was dead.
Dead! Oh, those were bitter hours;
Yet within my soul there dwelt
A warning, and while others mourned him,
Something like a hope I felt.

His was no weak life as mine was,
But a life, so full and strong
No, I could not think he perished
Nameless, 'mid a conquered throng.
How she drooped! Years passed; no tidings
Came, and yet that little flame
Of strange hope within my spirit
Still burnt on, and lived the same.

Ah! my child, our hearts will fail us,
When to us they strongest seem;
I can look back on those hours
As a fearful, evil dream.
She had long despaired; what wonder
That her heart had turned to mine?
Earthly loves are deep and tender,
Not eternal and divine!

Can I say how bright a future
Rose before my soul that day?
Oh, so strange, so sweet, so tender
And I had to turn away.
Hard and terrible the struggle,
For the pain not mine alone;
I called back my Brother's spirit,
And I bade him claim his own.

Told her, now I dared to do it
That I felt the day would rise
When he would return to gladden
My weak heart and her bright eyes.
And I pleaded, pleaded sternly
In his name, and for his sake:
Now, I can speak calmly of it,
Then, I thought my heart would break.

Soon, ah, Love had not deceived me,
(Love's true instincts never err,)
Wounded, weak, escaped from prison,
He returned to me; to her.
I could thank God that bright morning,
When I felt my Brother's gaze,
That my heart was true and loyal,
As in our old boyish days.

Bought by wounds and deeds of daring,
Honours he had brought away;
Glory crowned his name, my Brother's;
Mine too! we were one that day.
Since the crown on him had fallen,

"VICTOR IN A NOBLE STRIFE,"
I could live and die contented
With my poor ignoble life.

Well, my darling, almost weary
Of my story? Wait awhile;
For the rest is only joyful;
I can tell it with a smile.
One bright promise still was left me,
Wound so close about my soul,
That, as one by one had failed me,
This dream now absorbed the whole.

"SINGER OF A NOBLE POEM,"
Ah, my darling, few and rare
Burn the glorious names of Poets,
Like stars in the purple air.
That too, and I glory in it,
That great gift my Godfrey won;
I have my dear share of honour,
Gained by that beloved one.

One day shall my darling read it;
Now she cannot understand
All the noble thoughts, that lighten
Through the genius of the land.
I am proud to be his brother,
Proud to think that hope was true;
Though I longed and strove so vainly,
What I failed in, he could do.

I was long before I knew it,
Longer ere I felt it so;
Then I strung my rhymes together
Only for the poor and low.
And, it pleases me to know it,
(For I love them well indeed,)
They care for my humble verses,
Fitted for their humble need.

And, it cheers my heart to bear it,
Where the far-off settlers roam,
My poor words are sung and cherished,
Just because they speak of Home.
And the little children sing them,
(That, I think, has pleased me best,)
Often, too, the dying love them,
For they tell of Heaven and rest.

So my last vain dream has faded;
(Such as I to think of fame!)

Yet I will not say it failed me,
For it crowned my Godfrey's name.
No; my Angel did not cheat me,
For my long life has been blest;
He did give me Love and Sorrow,
He will bring me Light and Rest.

A WOMAN'S QUESTION

Before I trust my Fate to thee,
Or place my hand in thine,
Before I let thy Future give
Colour and form to mine,
Before I peril all for thee, question thy soul to-night for me.

I break all slighter bonds, nor feel
A shadow of regret:
Is there one link within the Past,
That holds thy spirit yet?
Or is thy Faith as clear and free as that which I can pledge to thee?

Does there within thy dimmest dreams
A possible future shine,
Wherein thy life could henceforth breathe,
Untouched, unshared by mine?
If so, at any pain or cost, oh, tell me before all is lost.

Look deeper still. If thou canst feel
Within thy inmost soul,
That thou hast kept a portion back,
While I have staked the whole;
Let no false pity spare the blow, but in true mercy tell me so.

Is there within thy heart a need
That mine cannot fulfil?
One chord that any other hand
Could better wake or still?
Speak now, lest at some future day my whole life wither and decay.

Lives there within thy nature bid
The demon-spirit Change,
Shedding a passing glory still
On all things new and strange?
It may not be thy fault alone but shield my heart against thy own.

Couldst thou withdraw thy hand one day
And answer to my claim,
That Fate, and that to-day's mistake,
Not thou had been to blame?

Some soothe their conscience thus: but thou, wilt surely warn and save me now.

Nay, answer not, I dare not hear,
The words would come too late;
Yet I would spare thee all remorse,
So, comfort thee, my Fate
Whatever on my heart may fall, remember I would risk it all!

THE THREE RULERS

I saw a Ruler take his stand
And trample on a mighty land;
The People crouched before his beck,
His iron heel was on their neck,
His name shone bright through blood and pain,
His sword flashed back their praise again.

I saw another Ruler rise
His words were noble, good, and wise;
With the calm sceptre of his pen
He ruled the minds and thoughts of men;
Some scoffed, some praised, while many heard,
Only a few obeyed his word.

Another Ruler then I saw
Love and sweet Pity were his law:
The greatest and the least had part
(Yet most the unhappy) in his heart
The People, in a mighty band,
Rose up, and drove him from the land!

A DEAD PAST

Spare her at least: look, you have taken from me
The Present, and I murmur not, nor moan;
The Future too, with all her glorious promise;
But do not leave me utterly alone.

Spare me the Past for, see, she cannot harm you,
She lies so white and cold, wrapped in her shroud;
All, all my own! and, trust me, I will hide her
Within my soul, nor speak to her aloud.

I folded her soft hands upon her bosom,
And strewed my flowers upon her, they still live
Sometimes I like to kiss her closed white eye-lids,
And think of all the joy she used to give.

Cruel indeed it were to take her from me;
She sleeps, she will not wake, no fear, again:
And so I laid her, such a gentle burthen,
Quietly on my heart to still its pain.

I do not think that any smiling Present,
Any vague Future, spite of all her charms,
Could ever rival her. You know you laid her,
Long years ago, then living, in my arms.

Leave her at least, while my tears fall upon her,
I dream she smiles, just as she did of yore;
As dear as ever to me, nay, it may be,
Even dearer still, since I have nothing more.

A DOUBTING HEART

Where are the swallows fled?
Frozen and dead,
Perchance upon some bleak and stormy shore.
Oh doubting heart!
Far over purple seas,
They wait, in sunny ease,
The balmy southern breeze,
To bring them to their northern homes once more.

Why must the flowers die?
Prisoned they lie
In the cold tomb, heedless of tears or rain.
Oh doubting heart!
They only sleep below
The soft white ermine snow,
While winter winds shall blow,
To breathe and smile upon you soon again.

The sun has hid its rays
These many days;
Will dreary hours never leave the earth?
Oh doubting heart!
The stormy clouds on high
Veil the same sunny sky,
That soon (for spring is nigh)
Shall wake the summer into golden mirth.

Fair hope is dead, and light
Is quenched in night.
What sound can break the silence of despair?
Oh doubting heart!

Thy sky is overcast,
Yet stars shall rise at last,
Brighter for darkness past,
And angels' silver voices stir the air.

A STUDENT

Over an ancient scroll I bent,
Steeping my soul in wise content,
Nor paused a moment, save to chide
A low voice whispering at my side.

I wove beneath the stars' pale shine
A dream, half human, half divine;
And shook off (not to break the charm)
A little hand laid on my arm.

I read; until my heart would glow
With the great deeds of long ago;
Nor heard, while with those mighty dead,
Pass to and fro a faltering tread.

On the old theme I pondered long
The struggle between right and wrong;
I could not check such visions high,
To soothe a little quivering sigh.

I tried to solve the problem, Life;
Dreaming of that mysterious strife,
How could I leave such reasonings wise,
To answer two blue pleading eyes?

I strove how best to give, and when,
My blood to save my fellow-men
How could I turn aside, to look
At snowdrops laid upon my book?

Now Time has fled, the world is strange,
Something there is of pain and change;
My books lie closed upon the shelf;
I miss the old heart in myself.

I miss the sunbeams in my room
It was not always wrapped in gloom:
I miss my dreams, they fade so fast,
Or flit into some trivial past.

The great stream of the world goes by;
None care, or heed, or question, why

I, the lone student, cannot raise
My voice or hand as in old days.

No echo seems to wake again
My heart to anything but pain,
Save when a dream of twilight brings
The fluttering of an angel's wings!

A KNIGHT ERRANT

Though he lived and died among us,
Yet his name may be enrolled
With the knights whose deeds of daring
Ancient chronicles have told.

Still a stripling, he encountered
Poverty, and struggled long,
Gathering force from every effort,
Till he knew his arm was strong.

Then his heart and life he offered
To his radiant mistress, Truth;
Never thought, or dream, or faltering,
Marred the promise of his youth.

So he rode forth to defend her,
And her peerless worth proclaim;
Challenging each recreant doubter
Who aspersed her spotless name.

First upon his path stood Ignorance,
Hideous in his brutal might;
Hard the blows and long the battle
Ere the monster took to flight.

Then, with light and fearless spirit,
Prejudice he dared to brave;
Hunting back the lying craven
To her black sulphureous cave.

Followed by his servile minions,
Custom, the old Giant, rose;
Yet he, too, at last was conquered
By the good Knight's weighty blows.

Then he turned, and, flushed with victory
Struck upon the brazen shield
Of the world's great king, Opinion
And defied him to the field.

Once again he rose a conqueror,
And, though wounded in the fight,
With a dying smile of triumph
Saw that Truth had gained her right.

On his failing ear re-echoing
Came the shouting round her throne;
Little cared he that no future
With her name would link his own.

Spent with many a hard-fought battle,
Slowly ebbed his life away,
And the crowd that flocked to greet her
Trampled on him where he lay.

Gathering all his strength, he saw her
Crowned and reigning in her pride!
Looked his last upon her beauty,
Raised his eyes to God, and died.

LINGER, OH, GENTLE TIME

Linger, oh, gentle Time,
Linger, oh, radiant grace of bright To-day!
Let not the hours' chime
Call thee away,
But linger near me still with fond delay.

Linger, for thou art mine!
What dearer treasures can the future hold?
What sweeter flowers than thine
Can she unfold?
What secrets tell my heart thou hast not told?

Oh, linger in thy flight!
For shadows gather round, and should we part,
A dreary starless night
May fill my heart,
Then pause and linger yet ere thou depart.

Linger, I ask no more,
Thou art enough for ever, thou alone;
What future can restore,
When thou art flown,
All that I hold from thee and call my own?

I have seen a fiercer tempest,
Known a louder whirlwind blow;
I was wrecked off red Algiers,
Six-and-thirty years ago.
Young I was, and yet old seamen
Were not strong or calm as I;
While life held such treasures for me,
I felt sure I could not die.

Life I struggled for and saved it;
Life alone and nothing more;
Bruised, half dead, alone and helpless,
I was cast upon the shore.
I feared the pitiless rocks of Ocean;
So the great sea rose and then
Cast me from her friendly bosom,
On the pitiless hearts of men.

Gaunt and dreary ran the mountains,
With black gorges, up the land;
Up to where the lonely Desert
Spreads her burning, dreary sand:
In the gorges of the mountains,
On the plain beside the sea,
Dwelt my stern and cruel masters,
The black Moors of Barbary.

Ten long years I toiled among them,
Hopeless as I used to say;
Now I know Hope burnt within me
Fiercer, stronger, day by day:
Those dim years of toil and sorrow
Like one long dark dream appear;
One long day of weary waiting
Then each day was like a year.

How I cursed the land, my prison;
How I cursed the serpent sea
And the Demon Fate that showered
All her curses upon me;
I was mad, I think, God pardon
Words so terrible and wild
This voyage would have been my last one,
For I left a wife and child.

Never did one tender vision
Fade away before my sight,
Never once through all my slavery,
Burning day or dreary night;

In my soul it lived, and kept me,
Now I feel, from black despair,
And my heart was not quite broken,
While they lived and blest me there.

When at night my task was over,
I would hasten to the shore;
(All was strange and foreign inland,
Nothing I had known before;)
Strange looked the bleak mountain passes,
Strange the red glare and black shade,
And the Oleanders, waving
To the sound the fountains made.

Then I gazed at the great Ocean,
Till she grew a friend again;
And because she knew old England,
I forgave her all my pain:
So the blue still sky above me,
With its white clouds' fleecy fold,
And the glimmering stars, (though brighter,)
Looked like home and days of old.

And a calm would fall upon me,
Worn perhaps with work and pain,
The wild hungry longing left me,
And I was myself again:
Looking at the silver waters,
Looking up at the far sky,
Dreams of home and all I left there
Floated sorrowfully by.

A fair face, but pale with sorrow,
With blue eyes, brimful of tears,
And the little red mouth, quivering
With a smile, to hide its fears;
Holding out her baby towards me,
From the sky she looked on me;
So it was that last I saw her,
As the ship put out to sea.

Sometimes, (and a pang would seize me
That the years were floating on,)
I would strive to paint her, altered,
And the little baby gone:
She no longer young and girlish,
The child, standing by her knee,
And her face, more pale and saddened
With the weariness for me.

Then I saw, as night grew darker.

How she taught my child to pray,
Holding its small hands together,
For its father, far away;
And I felt her sorrow, weighing
Heavier on me than my own;
Pitying her blighted spring-time,
And her joy so early flown.

Till upon my hands (now hardened
With the rough, harsh toil of years)
Bitter drops of anguish falling,
Woke me from my dream, to tears;
Woke me as a slave, an outcast.
Leagues from home, across the deep;
So, though you may call it childish
So I sobbed myself to sleep.

Well, the years sped on, my Sorrow,
Calmer, and yet stronger grown,
Was my shield against all suffering,
Poorer, meaner, than her own.
Thus my cruel master's harshness
Fell upon me all in vain,
Yet the tale of what we suffered
Echoed back from main to main.

You have heard in a far country
Of a self-devoted band,
Vowed to rescue Christian captives
Pining in a foreign land.
And these gentle-hearted strangers
Year by year go forth from Rome,
In their hands the hard-earned ransom,
To restore some exiles home.

I was freed: they broke the tidings
Gently to me: but indeed
Hour by hour sped on, I knew not
What the words meant, I was freed!
Better so, perhaps; while sorrow
(More akin to earthly things)
Only strains the sad heart's fibres
Joy, bright stranger, breaks the strings.

Yet at last it rushed upon me,
And my heart beat full and fast;
What were now my years of waiting,
What was all the dreary past?
Nothing to the impatient throbbing
I must bear across the sea:
Nothing to the eternal hours

Still between my home and me!

How the voyage passed, I know not;
Strange it was once more to stand
With my countrymen around me,
And to clasp an English hand.
But, through all, my heart was dreaming
Of the first words I should hear,
In the gentle voice that echoed,
Fresh as ever, on my ear.

Should I see her start of wonder,
And the sudden truth arise,
Flushing all her face and lightening
The dimmed splendour of her eyes?
Oh! to watch the fear and doubting
Stir the silent depths of pain,
And the rush of joy, then melting
Into perfect peace again.

And the child! but why remember
Foolish fancies that I thought?
Every tree and every hedge-row
From the well-known past I brought:
I would picture my dear cottage,
See the crackling wood-fire burn,
And the two beside it seated,
Watching, waiting, my return.

So, at last we reached the harbour.
I remember nothing more
Till I stood, my sick heart throbbing,
With my hand upon the door.
There I paused, I heard her speaking;
Low, soft, murmuring words she said;
Then I first knew the dumb terror
I had had, lest she were dead.

It was evening in late autumn,
And the gusty wind blew chill;
Autumn leaves were falling round me,
And the red sun lit the hill.
Six-and-twenty years are vanished
Since then, I am old and grey,
But I never told to mortal
What I saw, until this day.

She was seated by the fire,
In her arms she held a child,
Whispering baby-words caressing,
And then, looking up, she smiled:

Smiled on him who stood beside her
Oh! the bitter truth was told,
In her look of trusting fondness
I had seen the look of old!

But she rose and turned towards me
(Cold and dumb I waited there)
With a shriek of fear and terror,
And a white face of despair.
He had been an ancient comrade
Not a single word we said,
While we gazed upon each other,
He the living: I the dead!

I drew nearer, nearer to her,
And I took her trembling hand,
Looking on her white face, looking
That her heart might understand
All the love and all the pity
That my lips refused to say
I thank God no thought save sorrow
Rose in our crushed hearts that day.

Bitter tears that desolate moment,
Bitter, bitter tears we wept,
We three broken hearts together,
While the baby smiled and slept.
Tears alone, no words were spoken,
Till he, till her husband said
That my boy, (I had forgotten
The poor child,) that he was dead.

Then at last I rose, and, turning,
Wrung his hand, but made no sign;
And I stooped and kissed her forehead
Once more, as if she were mine.
Nothing of farewell I uttered,
Save in broken words to pray
That God would ever guard and bless her
Then in silence passed away.

Over the great restless ocean
Six-and-twenty years I roam;
All my comrades, old and weary,
Have gone back to die at home.
Home! yes, I shall reach a haven,
I, too, shall reach home and rest;
I shall find her waiting for me
With our baby on her breast.

LIFE AND DEATH

"What is Life, Father?"
"A Battle, my child,
Where the strongest lance may fail,
Where the wariest eyes may be beguiled,
And the stoutest heart may quail.
Where the foes are gathered on every hand,
And rest not day or night,
And the feeble little ones must stand
In the thickest of the fight."

"What is Death, Father?"
"The rest, my child,
When the strife and the toil are o'er;
The Angel of God, who, calm and mild,
Says we need fight no more;
Who, driving away the demon band,
Bids the din of the battle cease;
Takes banner and spear from our failing hand,
And proclaims an eternal Peace."

"Let me die, Father! I tremble and fear
To yield in that terrible strife!"

"The crown must be won for Heaven, dear,
In the battle-field of life:
My child, though thy foes are strong and tried,
He loveth the weak and small;
The Angels of Heaven are on thy side,
And God is over all!"

NOW

Rise! for the day is passing,
And you lie dreaming on;
The others have buckled their armour,
And forth to the fight are gone:
A place in the ranks awaits you,
Each man has some part to play;
The Past and the Future are nothing,
In the face of the stern To-day.

Rise from your dreams of the Future
Of gaining some hard-fought field;
Of storming some airy fortress,
Or bidding some giant yield;
Your Future has deeds of glory,

Of honour (God grant it may!)
But your arm will never be stronger,
Or the need so great as To-day.

Rise! if the Past detains you,
Her sunshine and storms forget;
No chains so unworthy to hold you
As those of a vain regret:
Sad or bright, she is lifeless ever,
Cast her phantom arms away,
Nor look back, save to learn the lesson
Of a nobler strife To-day.

Rise! for the day is passing:
The sound that you scarcely hear
Is the enemy marching to battle
Arise! for the foe is here!
Stay not to sharpen your weapons,
Or the hour will strike at last,
When, from dreams of a coming battle,
You may wake to find it past!

CLEANSING FIRES

Let thy gold be cast in the furnace,
Thy red gold, precious and bright,
Do not fear the hungry fire,
With its caverns of burning light:
And thy gold shall return more precious,
Free from every spot and stain;
For gold must be tried by fire,
As a heart must be tried by pain!

In the cruel fire of Sorrow
Cast thy heart, do not faint or wail;
Let thy hand be firm and steady,
Do not let thy spirit quail:
But wait till the trial is over,
And take thy heart again;
For as gold is tried by fire,
So a heart must be tried by pain!

I shall know by the gleam and glitter
Of the golden chain you wear,
By your heart's calm strength in loving,
Of the fire they have had to bear.
Beat on, true heart, forever;
Shine bright, strong golden chain;
And bless the cleansing fire,

And the furnace of living pain!

THE VOICE OF THE WIND

Let us throw more logs on the fire!
We have need of a cheerful light,
And close round the hearth to gather,
For the wind has risen to-night.
With the mournful sound of its wailing
It has checked the children's glee,
And it calls with a louder clamour
Than the clamour of the sea.
Hark to the voice of the wind!

Let us listen to what it is saying,
Let us hearken to where it has been;
For it tells, in its terrible crying,
The fearful sights it has seen.
It clatters loud at the casements,
Round the house it hurries on,
And shrieks with redoubled fury,
When we say "The blast is gone!"
Hark to the voice of the wind!

It has been on the field of battle,
Where the dying and wounded lie;
And it brings the last groan they uttered,
And the ravenous vulture's cry.
It has been where the icebergs were meeting,
And closed with a fearful crash;
On shores where no foot has wandered,
It has heard the waters dash.
Hark to the voice of the wind!

It has been on the desolate ocean,
When the lightning struck the mast;
It has heard the cry of the drowning,
Who sank as it hurried past;
The words of despair and anguish,
That were heard by no living ear;
The gun that no signal answered:
It brings them all to us here.
Hark to the voice of the wind!

It has been on the lonely moorland,
Where the treacherous snow-drift lies,
Where the traveller, spent and weary,
Gasped fainter and fainter cries;
It has heard the bay of the bloodhounds,

On the track of the hunted slave,
The lash and the curse of the master,
And the groan that the captive gave.
Hark to the voice of the wind!

It has swept through the gloomy forest,
Where the sledge was urged to its speed,
Where the howling wolves were rushing
On the track of the panting steed.
Where the pool was black and lonely,
It caught up a splash and a cry
Only the bleak sky heard it,
And the wind as it hurried by.
Hark to the voice of the wind!

Then throw more logs on the fire,
Since the air is bleak and cold,
And the children are drawing nigher,
For the tales that the wind has told.
So closer and closer gather
Round the red and crackling light;
And rejoice (while the wind is blowing)
We are safe and warm to-night.
Hark to the voice of the wind!

TREASURES

Let me count my treasures,
All my soul holds dear,
Given me by dark spirits
Whom I used to fear.

Through long days of anguish,
And sad nights, did Pain
Forge my shield, Endurance,
Bright and free from stain!

Doubt, in misty caverns,
'Mid dark horrors sought,
Till my peerless jewel,
Faith to me she brought.

Sorrow, that I wearied
Should remain so long,
Wreathed my starry glory,
The bright Crown of Song.

Strife, that racked my spirit,
Without hope or rest,

Left the blooming flower,
Patience, on my breast.

Suffering, that I dreaded,
Ignorant of her charms,
Laid the fair child, Pity,
Smiling, in my arms.

So I count my treasures,
Stored in days long past
And I thank the givers,
Whom I know at last!

SHINING STARS

Shine, ye stars of heaven,
On a world of pain!
See old Time destroying
All our hoarded gain;
All our sweetest flowers,
Every stately shrine,
All our hard-earned glory,
Every dream divine!

Shine, ye stars of heaven,
On the rolling years!
See how Time, consoling,
Dries the saddest tears,
Bids the darkest storm-clouds
Pass in gentle rain;
While upspring in glory,
Flowers and dreams again!

Shine, ye stars of heaven,
On a world of fear!
See how Time, avenging,
Bringeth judgment here;
Weaving ill-won honours
To a fiery crown;
Bidding hard hearts perish;
Casting proud hearts down.

Shine, ye stars of heaven,
On the hours' slow flight!
See how Time, rewarding,
Gilds good deeds with light;
Pays with kingly measure;
Brings earth's dearest prize;
Or, crowned with rays diviner,

Bids the end arise!

WAITING

"Wherefore dwell so sad and lonely,
By the desolate sea-shore,
With the melancholy surges
Beating at your cottage door?

"You shall dwell beside the castle
Shadowed by our ancient trees;
And your life shall pass on gently,
Cared for, and in rest and ease."

"Lady, one who loved me dearly
Sailed for distant lands away;
And I wait here his returning
Hopefully from day to day.

"To my door I bring my spinning,
Watching every ship I see;
Waiting, hoping, till the sunset
Fades into the western sea.

"After sunset, at my casement,
Still I place a signal light;
He will see its well-known shining
Should his ship return at night.

"Lady, see your infant smiling,
With its flaxen curling hair
I remember when your mother
Was a baby just as fair.

"I was watching then, and hoping:
Years have brought great change to all;
To my neighbours in their cottage,
To you nobles at the hall.

"Not to me, for I am waiting,
And the years have fled so fast,
I must look at you to tell me
That a weary time has past!

"When I hear a footstep coming
On the shingle, years have fled
Yet amid a thousand others,
I shall know his quick, light tread.

"When I hear (to-night it may be)
Someone pausing at my door,
I shall know the gay soft accents,
Heard and welcomed oft before!

"So each day I am more hopeful,
He may come before the night:
Every sunset I feel surer
He must come ere morning light.

"Then I thank you, noble lady,
But I cannot do your will:
Where he left me, he must find me.
Waiting, watching, hoping, still!"

THE CRADLE SONG OF THE POOR

Hush! I cannot bear to see thee
Stretch thy tiny hands in vain;
Dear, I have no bread to give thee,
Nothing, child, to ease thy pain!
When God sent thee first to bless me,
Proud, and thankful too, was I;
Now, my darling I, thy mother,
Almost long to see thee die.
Sleep, my darling, thou art weary;
God is good, but life is dreary.

I have watched thy beauty fading,
And thy strength sink day by day;
Soon, I know, will Want and Fever
Take thy little life away.
Famine makes thy father reckless,
Hope has left both him and me;
We could suffer all, my baby,
Had we but a crust for thee.
Sleep, my darling, thou art weary;
God is good, but life is dreary.

Better thou shouldst perish early,
Starve so soon, my darling one,
Than in helpless sin and sorrow
Vainly live, as I have done.
Better that thy angel spirit
With my joy, my peace, were flown,
Than thy heart grew cold and careless,
Reckless, hopeless, like my own.
Sleep, my darling, thou art weary;
God is good, but life is dreary.

I am wasted, dear, with hunger,
And my brain is all opprest,
I have scarcely strength to press thee,
Wan and feeble, to my breast.
Patience, baby, God will help us,
Death will come to thee and me,
He will take us to his Heaven,
Where no want or pain can be.
Sleep, my darling, thou art weary;
God is good, but life is dreary.

Such the plaint that, late and early,
Did we listen, we might hear
Close beside us, but the thunder
Of a city dulls our ear.
Every heart, as God's bright Angel,
Can bid one such sorrow cease;
God has glory when his children
Bring his poor ones joy and peace!
Listen, nearer while she sings
Sounds the fluttering of wings!

BE STRONG

Be strong to hope, oh Heart!
Though day is bright,
The stars can only shine
In the dark night.
Be strong, oh Heart of mine,
Look towards the light!

Be strong to bear, oh Heart!
Nothing is vain:
Strive not, for life is care,
And God sends pain,
Heaven is above, and there
Rest will remain!

Be strong to love, oh Heart!
Love knows not wrong,
Didst thou love, creatures even,
Life were not long;
Didst thou love God in Heaven,
Thou wouldst be strong!

GOD'S GIFTS

God gave a gift to Earth:—a child,
Weak, innocent, and undefiled,
Opened its ignorant eyes and smiled.

It lay so helpless, so forlorn,
Earth took it coldly and in scorn,
Cursing the day when it was born.

She gave it first a tarnished name,
For heritage, a tainted fame,
Then cradled it in want and shame.

All influence of Good or Right,
All ray of God's most holy light,
She curtained closely from its sight.

Then turned her heart, her eyes away,
Ready to look again, the day
Its little feet began to stray.

In dens of guilt the baby played,
Where sin, and sin alone, was made
The law that all around obeyed.

With ready and obedient care,
He learnt the tasks they taught him there;
Black sin for lesson, oaths for prayer.

Then Earth arose, and, in her might,
To vindicate her injured right,
Thrust him in deeper depths of night.

Branding him with a deeper brand
Of shame, he could not understand,
The felon outcast of the land.

God gave a gift to Earth:—a child,
Weak, innocent, and undefiled,
Opened its ignorant eyes and smiled.

And Earth received the gift, and cried
Her joy and triumph far and wide,
Till echo answered to her pride.

She blest the hour when first he came
To take the crown of pride and fame,
Wreathed through long ages for his name.

Then bent her utmost art and skill
To train the supple mind and will,

And guard it from a breath of ill.

She strewed his morning path with flowers,
And Love, in tender dropping showers,
Nourished the blue and dawning hours.

She shed, in rainbow hues of light,
A halo round the Good and Right,
To tempt and charm the baby's sight.

And every step, of work or play.
Was lit by some such dazzling ray,
Till morning brightened into day.

And then the World arose, and said
Let added honours now be shed
On such a noble heart and head!

O World, both gifts were pure and bright,
Holy and sacred in God's sight:—
God will judge them and thee aright!

A TOMB IN GHENT

A smiling look she had, a figure slight,
With cheerful air, and step both quick and light;
A strange and foreign look the maiden bore,
That suited the quaint Belgian dress she wore
Yet the blue fearless eyes in her fair face,
And her soft voice told her of English race;
And ever, as she flitted to and fro,
She sang, (or murmured, rather,) soft and low,
Snatches of song, as if she did not know
That she was singing, but the happy load
Of dream and thought thus from her heart o'erflowed:
And while on household cares she passed along,
The air would bear me fragments of her song;
Not such as village maidens sing, and few
The framers of her changing music knew;
Chants such as heaven and earth first heard of when
The master Palestrina held the pen.
But I with awe had often turned the page,
Yellow with time, and half defaced by age,
And listened, with an ear not quite unskilled,
While heart and soul to the grand echo thrilled;
And much I marvelled, as her cadence fell
From the Laudate, that I knew so well,
Into Scarlatti's minor fugue, how she
Had learned such deep and solemn harmony.

But what she told I set in rhyme, as meet
To chronicle the influence, dim and sweet,
'Neath which her young and innocent life had grown:
Would that my words were simple as her own.

Many years since, an English workman went
Over the seas, to seek a home in Ghent,
Where English skill was prized; nor toiled in vain;
Small, yet enough, his hard-earned daily gain.
He dwelt alone, in sorrow, or in pride.
He mixed not with the workers by his side;
He seemed to care but for one present joy
To tend, to watch, to teach his sickly boy.
Severe to all beside, yet for the child
He softened his rough speech to soothings mild;
For him he smiled, with him each day he walked
Through the dark gloomy streets; to him he talked
Of home, of England, and strange stories told
Of English heroes in the days of old;
And, (when the sunset gilded roof and spire,)
The marvellous tale which never seemed to tire:
How the gilt dragon, glaring fiercely down
From the great belfry, watching all the town,
Was brought, a trophy of the wars divine,
By a Crusader from far Palestine,
And given to Bruges; and how Ghent arose,
And how they struggled long as deadly foes,
Till Ghent, one night, by a brave soldier's skill,
Stole the great dragon; and she keeps it still.
One day the dragon, so 'tis said, will rise,
Spread his bright wines, and glitter in the skies.
And over desert lands and azure seas,
Will seek his home 'mid palm and cedar trees.
So, as he passed the belfry every day,
The boy would look if it were flown away;
Each day surprised to find it watching there,
Above him, as he crossed the ancient square,
To seek the great cathedral, that had grown
A home for him, mysterious and his own.

Dim with dark shadows of the ages past,
St. Bavon stands, solemn and rich and vast;
The slender pillars, in long vistas spread,
Like forest arches meet and close o'erhead;
So high that, like a weak and doubting prayer,
Ere it can float to the carved angels there,
The silver clouded incense faints in air:
Only the organ's voice, with peal on peal,
Can mount to where those far-off angels kneel.
Here the pale boy, beneath a low side-arch,
Would listen to its solemn chant or march;

Folding his little hands, his simple prayer
Melted in childish dreams, and both in air:
While the great organ over all would roll,
Speaking strange secrets to his innocent soul,
Bearing on eagle-wings the great desire
Of all the kneeling throng, and piercing higher
Than aught but love and prayer can reach, until
Only the silence seemed to listen still;
Or gathering like a sea still more and more,
Break in melodious waves at heaven's door,
And then fall, slow and soft, in tender rain,
Upon the pleading longing hearts again.

Then he would watch the rosy sunlight glow,
That crept along the marble floor below,
Passing, as life does, with the passing hours,
Now by a shrine all rich with gems and flowers,
Now on the brazen letters of a tomb,
Then, leaving it again to shade and gloom,
And creeping on, to show, distinct and quaint,
The kneeling figure of some marble saint:
Or lighting up the carvings strange and rare,
That told of patient toil, and reverent care;
Ivy that trembled on the spray, and ears,
Of heavy corn, and slender bulrush spears,
And all the thousand tangled weeds that grow
In summer, where the silver rivers flow;
And demon-heads grotesque, that seemed to glare
In impotent wrath on all the beauty there:
Then the gold rays up pillared shaft would climb,
And so be drawn to heaven, at evening time.
And deeper silence, darker shadows flowed
On all around, only the windows glowed
With blazoned glory, like the shields of light
Archangels bear, who, armed with love and might,
Watch upon heaven's battlements at night.
Then all was shade; the silver lamps that gleamed,
Lost in the daylight, in the darkness seemed
Like sparks of fire in the dim aisles to shine,
Or trembling stars before each separate shrine.
Grown half afraid, the child would leave them there,
And come out, blinded by the noisy glare
That burst upon him from the busy square.

The church was thus his home for rest or play,
And as he came and went again each day,
The pictured faces that he knew so well,
Seemed to smile on him welcome and farewell.
But holier, and dearer far than all,
One sacred spot his own he loved to call;
Save at mid-day, half-hidden by the gloom;

The people call it The White Maiden's Tomb:
For there she stands; her folded hands are pressed
Together, and laid softly on her breast,
As if she waited but a word to rise
From the dull earth, and pass to the blue skies;
Her lips expectant part, she holds her breath,
As listening for the angel voice of death.
None know how many years have seen her so,
Or what the name of her who sleeps below.
And here the child would come, and strive to trace,
Through the dim twilight, the pure gentle face
He loved so well, and here he oft would bring
Some violet blossom of the early spring;
And climbing softly by the fretted stand,
Not to disturb her, lay it in her hand;
Or, whispering a soft loving message sweet,
Would stoop and kiss the little marble feet.
So, when the organ's pealing music rang,
He thought amid the gloom the Maiden sang;
With reverent simple faith by her he knelt,
And fancied what she thought, and what she felt.
"Glory to God," re-echoed from her voice,
And then his little spirit would rejoice;
Or when the Requiem sobbed upon the air,
His baby tears dropped with her mournful prayer.

So years fled on, while childish fancies past,
The childish love and simple faith could last.
The artist-soul awoke in him, the flame
Of genius, like the light of Heaven, came
Upon his brain, and (as it will, if true)
It touched his heart and lit his spirit, too
His father saw, and with a proud content
Let him forsake the toil where he had spent
His youth's first years, and on one happy day
Of pride, before the old man passed away,
He stood with quivering lips, and the big tears
Upon his cheek, and heard the dream of years
Living and speaking to his very heart
The low hushed murmur at the wondrous art
Of him, who with young trembling fingers made
The great church-organ answer as he played;
And, as the uncertain sound grew full and strong,
Rush with harmonious spirit-wings along,
And thrill with master-power the breathless throng.

The old man died, and years passed on, and still
The young musician bent his heart and will
To his dear toil. St. Bavon now had grown
More dear to him, and even more his own;
And as he left it every night he prayed

A moment by the archway in the shade,
Kneeling once more within the sacred gloom
Where the White Maiden watched upon her tomb.
His hopes of travel and a world-wide fame,
Cold Time had sobered, and his fragile frame;
Content at last only in dreams to roam,
Away from the tranquillity of home;
Content that the poor dwellers by his side
Saw in him but the gentle friend and guide,
The patient counsellor in the poor strife
And petty details of their common life,
Who comforted where woe and grief might fall,
Nor slighted any pain or want as small,
But whose great heart took in and felt for all.

Still he grew famous, many came to be
His pupils in the art of harmony.
One day a voice floated so pure and free
Above his music, that he turned to see
What angel sang, and saw before his eyes,
What made his heart leap with a strange surprise,
His own White Maiden, calm, and pure, and mild,
As in his childish dreams she sang and smiled;
Her eyes raised up to Heaven, her lips apart,
And music overflowing from her heart.
But the faint blush that tinged her cheek betrayed
No marble statue, but a living maid;
Perplexed and startled at his wondering look,
Her rustling score of Mozart's Sanctus shook;
The uncertain notes, like birds within a snare,
Fluttered and died upon the trembling air.

Days passed; each morning saw the maiden stand,
Her eyes cast down, her lesson in her hand,
Eager to study, never weary, while
Repaid by the approving word or smile
Of her kind master; days and months fled on;
One day the pupil from the choir was gone;
Gone to take light, and joy, and youth once more,
Within the poor musician's humble door;
And to repay, with gentle happy art,
The debt so many owed his generous heart.
And now, indeed, was one who knew and felt
That a great gift of God within him dwelt;
One who could listen, who could understand,
Whose idle work dropped from her slackened hand,
While with wet eyes entranced she stood, nor knew
How the melodious winged hours flew;
Who loved his art as none had loved before,
Yet prized the noble tender spirit more.
While the great organ brought from far and near

Lovers of harmony to praise and hear,
Unmarked by aught save what filled every day,
Duty, and toil, and rest, years passed away:
And now by the low archway in the shade
Beside her mother knelt a little maid,
Who, through the great cathedral learned to roam,
Climb to the choir, and bring her father home;
And stand, demure and solemn by his side,
Patient till the last echo softly died;
Then place her little hand in his, and go
Down the dark winding stair to where below
The mother knelt, within the gathering gloom
Waiting and praying by the Maiden's Tomb.

So their life went, until, one winter's day,
Father and child came there alone to pray
The mother, gentle soul, had fled away!
Their life was altered now, and yet the child
Forgot her passionate grief in time, and smiled,
Half wondering why, when spring's fresh breezes came,
To see her father was no more the same.
Half guessing at the shadow of his pain,
And then contented if he smiled again,
A sad cold smile, that passed in tears away,
As re-assured she ran once more to play.
And now each year that added grace to grace,
Fresh bloom and sunshine to the young girl's face,
Brought a strange light in the musician's eyes,
As if he saw some starry hope arise,
Breaking upon the midnight of sad skies.
It might be so: more feeble year by year,
The wanderer to his resting-place drew near.
One day the Gloria he could play no more,
Echoed its grand rejoicing as of yore;
His hands were clasped, his weary head was laid,
Upon the tomb where the White Maiden prayed:
Where the child's love first dawned, his soul first spoke,
The old man's heart there throbbed its last and broke.
The grave cathedral that had nursed his youth,
Had helped his dreaming, and had taught him truth,
Had seen his boyish grief and baby tears,
And watched the sorrows and the joys of years,
Had lit his fame and hope with sacred rays,
And consecrated sad and happy days
Had blessed his happiness, and soothed his pain,
Now took her faithful servant home again.

He rests in peace: some travellers mention yet
An organist whose name they all forget.
He has a holier and a nobler fame
By poor men's hearths, who love and bless the name

Of a kind friend; and in low tones to-day,
Speak tenderly of him who passed away.
Too poor to help the daughter of their friend,
They grieved to see the little pittance end;
To see her toil and strive with cheerful heart,
To bear the lonely orphan's struggling part;
They grieved to see her go at last alone
To English kinsmen she had never known:
And here she came; the foreign girl soon found
Welcome, and love, and plenty all around,
And here she pays it back with earnest will,
By well-taught housewife watchfulness and skill;
Deep in her heart she holds her father's name,
And tenderly and proudly keeps his fame;
And while she works with thrifty Belgian care,
Past dreams of childhood float upon the air;
Some strange old chant, or solemn Latin hymn,
That echoed through the old cathedral dim,
When as a little child each day she went
To kneel and pray by an old tomb in Ghent.

THE ANGEL OF DEATH

Why shouldst thou fear the beautiful angel, Death,
Who waits thee at the portals of the skies,
Ready to kiss away thy struggling breath,
Ready with gentle hand to close thine eyes?

How many a tranquil soul has passed away,
Fled gladly from fierce pain and pleasures dim,
To the eternal splendour of the day;
And many a troubled heart still calls for him.

Spirits too tender for the battle here
Have turned from life, its hopes, its fears, its charms;
And children, shuddering at a world so drear,
Have smiling passed away into his arms.

He whom thou fearest will, to ease its pain,
Lay his cold hand upon thy aching heart:
Will soothe the terrors of thy troubled brain,
And bid the shadow of earth's grief depart.

He will give back what neither time, nor might,
Nor passionate prayer, nor longing hope restore.
(Dear as to long blind eyes recovered sight,)
He will give back those who are gone before.

Oh, what were life, if life were all? Thine eyes

Are blinded by their tears, or thou wouldst see
Thy treasures wait thee in the far-off skies,
And Death, thy friend, will give them all to thee.

A DREAM

All yesterday I was spinning,
Sitting alone in the sun;
And the dream that I spun was so lengthy,
It lasted till day was done.

I heeded not cloud or shadow
That flitted over the hill,
Or the humming-bees, or the swallows,
Or the trickling of the rill.

I took the threads for my spinning,
All of blue summer air,
And a flickering ray of sunlight
Was woven in here and there.

The shadows grew longer and longer,
The evening wind passed by,
And the purple splendour of sunset
Was flooding the western sky.

But I could not leave my spinning,
For so fair my dream had grown.
I heeded not, hour by hour,
How the silent day had flown.

At last the grey shadows fell round me,
And the night came dark and chill,
And I rose and ran down the valley,
And left it all on the hill.

I went up the hill this morning
To the place where my spinning lay
There was nothing but glistening dewdrops
Remained of my dream to-day.

THE PRESENT

Do not crouch to-day, and worship
The old Past, whose life is fled,
Hush your voice to tender reverence;
Crowned he lies, but cold and dead:

For the Present reigns our monarch,
With an added weight of hours;
Honour her, for she is mighty!
Honour her, for she is ours!

See the shadows of his heroes
Girt around her cloudy throne;
Every day the ranks are strengthened
By great hearts to him unknown;
Noble things the great Past promised,
Holy dreams, both strange and new;
But the Present shall fulfil them,
What he promised, she shall do.

She inherits all his treasures,
She is heir to all his fame,
And the light that lightens round her
Is the lustre of his name;
She is wise with all his wisdom,
Living on his grave she stands,
On her brow she bears his laurels,
And his harvest in her hands.

Coward, can she reign and conquer
If we thus her glory dim?
Let us fight for her as nobly
As our fathers fought for him.
God, who crowns the dying ages,
Bids her rule, and us obey
Bids us cast our lives before her,
Bids us serve the great To-day.

CHANGES

Mourn, O rejoicing heart!
The hours are flying;
Each one some treasure takes,
Each one some blossom breaks,
And leaves it dying;
The chill dark night draws near,
Thy sun will soon depart,
And leave thee sighing;
Then mourn, rejoicing heart,
The hours are flying!

Rejoice, O grieving heart!
The hours fly fast;
With each some sorrow dies,
With each some shadow flies,

Until at last
The red dawn in the east
Bids weary night depart,
And pain is past.
Rejoice then, grieving heart,
The hours fly fast!

STRIVE, WAIT, AND PRAY

Strive; yet I do not promise
The prize you dream of to-day
Will not fade when you think to grasp it,
And melt in your hand away;
But another and holier treasure,
You would now perchance disdain,
Will come when your toil is over,
And pay you for all your pain.

Wait; yet I do not tell you
The hour you long for now,
Will not come with its radiance vanished,
And a shadow upon its brow;
Yet far through the misty future,
With a crown of starry light,
An hour of joy you know not
Is winging her silent flight.

Pray; though the gift you ask for
May never comfort your fears,
May never repay your pleading,
Yet pray, and with hopeful tears;
An answer, not that you long for,
But diviner, will come one day,
Your eyes are too dim to see it,
Yet strive, and wait, and pray.

A LAMENT FOR THE SUMMER

Moan, oh ye Autumn Winds!
Summer has fled,
The flowers have closed their tender leaves and die;
The Lily's gracious head
All low must lie,
Because the gentle Summer now is dead.

Grieve, oh ye Autumn Winds!
Summer lies low;

The rose's trembling leaves will soon be shed,
For she that loved her so,
Alas, is dead!
And one by one her loving children go.

Wail, oh ye Autumn Winds!
She lives no more,
The gentle Summer, with her balmy breath,
Still sweeter than before
When nearer death,
And brighter every day the smile she wore!

Mourn, mourn, oh Autumn Winds,
Lament and mourn;
How many half-blown buds must close and die;
Hopes with the Summer born
All faded lie,
And leave us desolate and Earth forlorn!

THE UNKNOWN GRAVE

No name to bid us know
Who rests below,
No word of death or birth,
Only the grass's wave,
Over a mound of earth,
Over a nameless grave.

Did this poor wandering heart
In pain depart?
Longing, but all too late,
For the calm home again,
Where patient watchers wait,
And still will wait in vain.

Did mourners come in scorn,
And thus forlorn,
Leave him, with grief and shame.
To silence and decay,
And hide the tarnished name
Of the unconscious clay?

It may be from his side
His loved ones died,
And last of some bright band,
(Together now once more,)
He sought his home, the land
Where they had gone before.

No matter, limes have made
As cool a shade,
And lingering breezes pass
As tenderly and slow,
As if beneath the grass
A monarch slept below.

No grief, though loud and deep,
Could stir that sleep;
And earth and heaven tell
Of rest that shall not cease,
Where the cold world's farewell
Fades into endless peace.

GIVE ME THY HEART

With echoing steps the worshippers
Departed one by one;
The organ's pealing voice was stilled,
The vesper hymn was done;
The shadows fell from roof and arch,
Dim was the incensed air,
One lamp alone with trembling ray,
Told of the Presence there!

In the dark church she knelt alone;
Her tears were falling fast;
"Help, Lord," she cried, "the shades of death
Upon my soul are cast!
Have I not shunned the path of sin,
And chosen the better part?"
What voice came through the sacred air?
"My child, give me thy Heart!"

"Have I not laid before Thy shrine
My wealth, oh Lord?" she cried;
"Have I kept aught of gems or gold,
To minister to pride?
Have I not bade youth's joys retire,
And vain delights depart?"
But sad and tender was the voice
"My child, give me thy Heart!"

"Have I not, Lord, gone day by day
Where Thy poor children dwell;
And carried help, and gold, and food?
Oh Lord, Thou knowest it well!
From many a house, from many a soul,
My hand bids care depart:"

More sad, more tender, was the voice
"My child, give me thy Heart!"

"Have I not worn my strength away
With fast and penance sore?
Have I not watched and wept?" she cried;
"Did Thy dear Saints do more?
Have I not gained Thy grace, oh Lord,
And won in Heaven my part?"
It echoed louder in her soul
"My child, give me thy Heart!"

"For I have loved thee with a love
No mortal heart can show;
A love so deep, my Saints in heaven
Its depths can never know:
When pierced and wounded on the Cross,
Man's sin and doom were mine,
I loved thee with undying love,
Immortal and divine!

"I love thee ere the skies were spread;
My soul bears all thy pains;
To gain thy love my sacred Heart
In earthly shrines remains:
Vain are thy offerings, vain thy sighs,
Without one gift divine,
Give it, my child, thy Heart to me,
And it shall rest in mine!"

In awe she listened, and the shade
Passed from her soul away;
In low and trembling voice she cried
"Lord, help me to obey!
Break Thou the chains of earth, oh Lord,
That bind and hold my heart;
Let it be Thine, and Thine alone,
Let none with Thee have part.

"Send down, oh Lord, Thy sacred fire!
Consume and cleanse the sin
That lingers still within its depths:
Let heavenly love begin.
That sacred flame Thy Saints have known,
Kindle, oh Lord, in me,
Thou above all the rest for ever,
And all the rest in Thee."

The blessing fell upon her soul;
Her angel by her side
Knew that the hour of peace was come;

Her soul was purified:
The shadows fell from roof and arch,
Dim was the incensed air
But Peace went with her as she left
The sacred Presence there!

THE WAYSIDE INN

A little past the village
The Inn stood, low and white;
Green shady trees behind it,
And an orchard on the right;
Where over the green paling
The red-cheeked apples hung,
As if to watch how wearily
The sign-board creaked and swung.

The heavy-laden branches,
Over the road hung low,
Reflected fruit or blossom
From the wayside well below;
Where children, drawing water,
Looked up and paused to see,
Amid the apple-branches,
A purple Judas Tree.

The road stretched winding onward
For many a weary mile
So dusty foot-sore wanderers
Would pause and rest awhile;
And panting horses halted,
And travellers loved to tell
The quiet of the wayside inn,
The orchard, and the well.

Here Maurice dwelt; and often
The sunburnt boy would stand
Gazing upon the distance,
And shading with his hand
His eyes, while watching vainly
For travellers, who might need
His aid to loose the bridle,
And tend the weary steed.

And once (the boy remembered
That morning, many a day
The dew lay on the hawthorn,
The bird sang on the spray)
A train of horsemen, nobler

Than he had seen before,
Up from the distance galloped,
And halted at the door.

Upon a milk-white pony,
Fit for a faery queen,
Was the loveliest little damsel
His eyes had ever seen:
A serving-man was holding
The leading rein, to guide
The pony and its mistress,
Who cantered by his side.

Her sunny ringlets round her
A golden cloud had made,
While her large hat was keeping
Her calm blue eyes in shade;
One hand held fast the silken reins
To keep her steed in check,
The other pulled his tangled mane,
Or stroked his glossy neck.

And as the boy brought water,
And loosed the rein, he heard
The sweetest voice that thanked him
In one low gentle word;
She turned her blue eyes from him,
Looked up, and smiled to see
The hanging purple blossoms
Upon the Judas Tree;

And showed it with a gesture,
Half pleading, half command,
Till he broke the fairest blossom,
And laid it in her hand;
And she tied it to her saddle
With a ribbon from her hair,
While her happy laugh rang gaily,
Like silver on the air.

But the champing steeds were rested
The horsemen now spurred on,
And down the dusty highway
They vanished and were gone.
Years passed, and many a traveller
Paused at the old inn-door,
But the little milk-white pony
And the child returned no more.

Years passed, the apple-branches
A deeper shadow shed;

And many a time the Judas Tree,
Blossom and leaf, lay dead;
When on the loitering western breeze
Came the bells' merry sound,
And flowery arches rose, and flags
And banners waved around.

Maurice stood there expectant:
The bridal train would stay
Some moments at the inn-door,
The eager watchers say;
They come, the cloud of dust draws near
'Mid all the state and pride,
He only sees the golden hair
And blue eyes of the bride.

The same, yet, ah, still fairer;
He knew the face once more
That bent above the pony's neck
Years past at that inn-door:
Her shy and smiling eyes looked round,
Unconscious of the place,
Unconscious of the eager gaze
He fixed upon her face.

He plucked a blossom from the tree
The Judas Tree and cast
Its purple fragrance towards the Bride,
A message from the Past.
The signal came, the horses plunged
Once more she smiled around:
The purple blossom in the dust
Lay trampled on the ground.

Again the slow years fleeted,
Their passage only known
By the height the Passion-flower
Around the porch had grown;
And many a passing traveller
Paused at the old inn-door,
But the bride, so fair and blooming,
The bride returned no more.

One winter morning, Maurice,
Watching the branches bare,
Rustling and waving dimly
In the grey and misty air,
Saw blazoned on a carriage
Once more the well-known shield,
The stars and azure fleurs-de-lis
Upon a silver field.

He looked, was that pale woman,
So grave, so worn, so sad,
The child, once young and smiling,
The bride, once fair and glad?
What grief had dimmed that glory,
And brought that dark eclipse
Upon her blue eyes' radiance,
And paled those trembling lips?

What memory of past sorrow,
What stab of present pain,
Brought that deep look of anguish,
That watched the dismal rain,
That watched (with the absent spirit
That looks, yet does not see)
The dead and leafless branches
Upon the Judas Tree.

The slow dark months crept onward
Upon their icy way,
'Till April broke in showers
And Spring smiled forth in May;
Upon the apple-blossoms
The sun shone bright again,
When slowly up the highway
Came a long funeral train.

The bells toiled slowly, sadly,
For a noble spirit fled;
Slowly, in pomp and honour,
They bore the quiet dead.
Upon a black-plumed charger
One rode, who held a shield,
Where stars and azure fleurs-de-lis
Shone on a silver field.

'Mid all that homage given
To a fluttering heart at rest,
Perhaps an honest sorrow
Dwelt only in one breast.
One by the inn-door standing
Watched with fast-dropping tears
The long procession passing,
And thought of bygone years,

The boyish, silent homage
To child and bride unknown,
The pitying tender sorrow
Kept in his heart alone,
Now laid upon the coffin

With a purple flower, might be
Told to the cold dead sleeper;
The rest could only see
A fragrant purple blossom,
Plucked from a Judas Tree.

VOICES OF THE PAST

You wonder that my tears should flow
In listening to that simple strain;
That those unskilful sounds should fill
My soul with joy and pain
How can you tell what thoughts it stirs
Within my heart again?

You wonder why that common phrase,
So all unmeaning to your ear,
Should stay me in my merriest mood,
And thrill my soul to hear
How can you tell what ancient charm
Has made me hold it dear?

You marvel that I turn away
From all those flowers so fair and bright,
And gaze at this poor herb, till tears
Arise and dim my sight
You cannot tell how every leaf
Breathes of a past delight.

You smile to see me turn and speak
With one whose converse you despise;
You do not see the dreams of old
That with his voice arise
How can you tell what links have made
Him sacred in my eyes?

Oh, these are Voices of the Past,
Links of a broken chain,
Wings that can bear me back to Times
Which cannot come again
Yet God forbid that I should lose
The echoes that remain!

THE DARK SIDE

Thou hast done well, perhaps,
To lift the bright disguise,

And lay the bitter truth
Before our shrinking eyes;
When evil crawls below
What seems so pure and fair,
Thine eyes are keen and true
To find the serpent there:
And yet I turn away;
Thy task is not divine
The evil angels look
On earth with eyes like thine.

Thou hast done well, perhaps,
To show how closely wound
Dark threads of sin and self
With our best deeds are found.
How great and noble hearts,
Striving for lofty aims,
Have still some earthly cord
A meaner spirit claims;
And yet, although thy task
Is well and fairly done,
Methinks for such as thou
There is a holier one.

Shadows there are, who dwell
Among us, yet apart,
Deaf to the claim of God,
Or kindly human heart;
Voices of earth and heaven
Call, but they turn away,
And Love, through such black night,
Can see no hope of day;
And yet, our eyes are dim,
And thine are keener far
Then gaze till thou canst see
The glimmer of some star.

The black stream flows along,
Whose waters we despise
Show us reflected there
Some fragment of the skies;
'Neath tangled thorns and briars,
(The task is fit for thee,)
Seek for the hidden flowers,
We are too blind to see;
Then will I thy great gift
A crown and blessing call;
Angels look thus on men,
And God sees good in all!

A FIRST SORROW

Arise! this day shall shine,
For evermore,
To thee a star divine,
On Time's dark shore.

Till now thy soul has been
All glad and gay:
Bid it awake, and look
At grief to-day!

No shade has come between
Thee and the sun;
Like some long childish dream
Thy life has run:

But now the stream has reached
A dark, deep sea,
And Sorrow, dim and crowned,
Is waiting thee.

Each of God's soldiers bears
A sword divine:
Stretch out thy trembling hands
To-day for thine!

To each anointed Priest
God's summons came:
Oh, Soul, he speaks to-day
And calls thy name.

Then, with slow reverent step,
And beating heart,
From out thy joyous days,
Thou must depart.

And, leaving all behind,
Come forth, alone,
To join the chosen band
Around the throne.

Raise up thine eyes, be strong,
Nor cast away
The crown, that God has given
Thy soul to-day!

Why wilt thou make bright music
Give forth a sound of pain?
Why wilt thou weave fair flowers
Into a weary chain?

Why turn each cool grey shadow
Into a world of fears?
Why say the winds are wailing?
Why call the dewdrops tears?

The voices of happy nature,
And the Heaven's sunny gleam,
Reprove thy sick heart's fancies,
Upbraid thy foolish dream.

Listen, and I will tell thee
The song Creation sings,
From the humming of bees in the heather,
To the flutter of angels' wings.

An echo rings forever,
The sound can never cease;
It speaks to God of glory,
It speaks to Earth of peace.

Not alone did angels sing it
To the poor shepherds' ear;
But the sphered Heavens chant it,
While listening ages hear.

Above thy peevish wailing
Rises that holy song;
Above Earth's foolish clamour,
Above the voice of wrong.

No creature of God's too lowly
To murmur peace and praise:
When the starry nights grow silent,
Then speak the sunny days.

So leave thy sick heart's fancies,
And lend thy little voice
To the silver song of glory
That bids the world rejoice.

GIVE

See the rivers flowing

Downwards to the sea,
Pouring all their treasures
Bountiful and free
Yet to help their giving
Hidden springs arise;
Or, if need be, showers
Feed them from the skies!

Watch the princely flowers
Their rich fragrance spread,
Load the air with perfumes,
From their beauty shed
Yet their lavish spending
Leaves them not in dearth,
With fresh life replenished
By their mother earth!

Give thy heart's best treasures
From fair Nature learn;
Give thy love and ask not,
Wait not a return!
And the more thou spendest
From thy little store,
With a double bounty,
God will give thee more.

MY JOURNAL

It is a dreary evening;
The shadows rise and fall:
With strange and ghostly changes,
They flicker on the wall.

Make the charred logs burn brighter;
I will show you, by their blaze,
The half-forgotten record
Of bygone things and days.

Bring here the ancient volume;
The clasp is old and worn,
The gold is dim and tarnished,
And the faded leaves are torn.

The dust has gathered on it
There are so few who care
To read what Time has written
Of joy and sorrow there.

Look at the first fair pages;

Yes, I remember all:
The joys now seem so trivial,
The griefs so poor and small.

Let us read the dreams of glory
That childish fancy made;
Turn to the next few pages,
And see how soon they fade.

Here, where still waiting, dreaming,
For some ideal Life,
The young heart all unconscious
Had entered on the strife.

See how this page is blotted:
What, could those tears be mine?
How coolly I can read you,
Each blurred and trembling line.

Now I can reason calmly,
And, looking back again,
Can see divinest meaning
Threading each separate pain.

Here strong resolve, how broken;
Rash hope, and foolish fear,
And prayers, which God in pity
Refused to grant or hear.

Nay, I will turn the pages
To where the tale is told
Of how a dawn diviner
Flushed the dark clouds with gold.

And see, that light has gilded
The story, nor shall set;
And, though in mist and shadow,
You know I see it yet.

Here, well, it does not matter,
I promised to read all;
I know not why I falter,
Or why my tears should fall;

You see each grief is noted;
Yet it was better so
I can rejoice to-day, the pain
Was over, long ago.

I read, my voice is failing,
But you can understand

How the heart beat that guided
This weak and trembling hand.

Pass over that long struggle,
Read where the comfort came,
Where the first time is written
Within the book your name.

Again it comes, and oftener,
Linked, as it now must be,
With all the joy or sorrow
That Life may bring to me.

So all the rest, you know it:
Now shut the clasp again,
And put aside the record
Of bygone hours of pain.

The dust shall gather on it,
I will not read it more:
Give me your hand, what was it
We were talking of before?

I know not why, but tell me
Of something gay and bright.
It is strange, my heart is heavy,
And my eyes are dim to-night.

A CHAIN

The bond that links our souls together;
Will it last through stormy weather?
Will it moulder and decay
As the long hours pass away?
Will it stretch if Fate divide us,
When dark and weary hours have tried us?
Oh, if it look too poor and slight
Let us break the links to-night!

It was not forged by mortal hands,
Or clasped with golden bars and bands;
Save thine and mine, no other eyes
The slender link can recognise:
In the bright light it seems to fade
And it is hidden in the shade;
While Heaven nor Earth have never heard,
Or solemn vow, or plighted word.

Yet what no mortal hand could make,

No mortal power can ever break:
What words or vows could never do,
No words or vows can make untrue;
And if to other hearts unknown
The dearer and the more our own,
Because too sacred and divine
For other eyes, save thine and mine.

And see, though slender, it is made
Of Love and Trust, and can they fade?
While, if too slight it seem, to bear
The breathings of the summer air,
We know that it could bear the weight
Of a most heavy heart of late,
And as each day and hour flew
The stronger for its burthen grew.

And, too, we know and feel again
It has been sanctified by pain,
For what God deigns to try with sorrow
He means not to decay to-morrow;
But through that fiery trial last
When earthly ties and bonds are past;
What slighter things dare not endure
Will make our Love more safe and pure.

Love shall be purified by Pain,
And Pain be soothed by Love again:
So let us now take heart and go
Cheerfully on, through joy and woe;
No change the summer sun can bring,
Or the inconstant skies of spring,
Or the bleak winter's stormy weather,
For we shall meet them, Love, together!

THE PILGRIMS

The way is long and dreary,
The path is bleak and bare;
Our feet are worn and weary,
But we will not despair.
More heavy was Thy burthen,
More desolate Thy way;
Oh Lamb of God who takest
The sin of the world away,
Have mercy on us.

The snows lie thick around us
In the dark and gloomy night;

And the tempest wails above us,
And the stars have hid their light;
But blacker was the darkness
Round Calvary's Cross that day;
Oh Lamb of God who takest
The sin of the world away,
Have mercy on us.

Our hearts are faint with sorrow,
Heavy and hard to bear;
For we dread the bitter morrow,
But we will not despair:
Thou knowest all our anguish,
And Thou wilt bid it cease,
Oh Lamb of God who takest
The sin of the world away,
Give us Thy Peace!

INCOMPLETENESS

Nothing resting in its own completeness
Can have worth or beauty: but alone
Because it leads and tends to farther sweetness,
Fuller, higher, deeper than its own.

Spring's real glory dwells not in the meaning,
Gracious though it be, of her blue hours;
But is hidden in her tender leaning
To the Summer's richer wealth of flowers.

Dawn is fair, because the mists fade slowly
Into Day, which floods the world with light;
Twilight's mystery is so sweet and holy
Just because it ends in starry Night.

Childhood's smiles unconscious graces borrow
From Strife, that in a far-off future lies;
And angel glances (veiled now by Life's sorrow)
Draw our hearts to some beloved eyes.

Life is only bright when it proceedeth
Towards a truer, deeper Life above;
Human Love is sweetest when it leadeth
To a more divine and perfect Love.

Learn the mystery of Progression duly:
Do not call each glorious change, Decay;
But know we only hold our treasures truly,
When it seems as if they passed away.

Nor dare to blame God's gifts for incompleteness;
In that want their beauty lies: they roll
Towards some infinite depth of love and sweetness,
Bearing onward man's reluctant soul.

A LEGEND OF BREGENZ

Girt round with rugged mountains
The fair Lake Constance lies;
In her blue heart reflected
Shine back the starry skies;
And, watching each white cloudlet
Float silently and slow,
You think a piece of Heaven
Lies on our earth below!

Midnight is there: and Silence,
Enthroned in Heaven, looks down
Upon her own calm mirror,
Upon a sleeping town:
For Bregenz, that quaint city
Upon the Tyrol shore,
Has stood above Lake Constance,
A thousand years and more.

Her battlements and towers,
From off their rocky steep,
Have cast their trembling shadow
For ages on the deep:
Mountain, and lake, and valley,
A sacred legend know,
Of how the town was saved, one night,
Three hundred years ago.

Far from her home and kindred,
A Tyrol maid had fled,
To serve in the Swiss valleys,
And toil for daily bread;
And every year that fleeted
So silently and fast,
Seemed to bear farther from her
The memory of the Past.

She served kind, gentle masters,
Nor asked for rest or change;
Her friends seemed no more new ones,
Their speech seemed no more strange;

And when she led her cattle
To pasture every day,
She ceased to look and wonder
On which side Bregenz lay.

She spoke no more of Bregenz,
With longing and with tears:
Her Tyrol home seemed faded
In a deep mist of years;
She heeded not the rumours
Of Austrian war and strife;
Each day she rose contented,
To the calm toils of life.

Yet, when her master's children
Would clustering round her stand,
She sang them ancient ballads
Of her own native land;
And when at morn and evening
She knelt before God's throne,
The accents of her childhood
Rose to her lips alone.

And so she dwelt: the valley
More peaceful year by year;
When suddenly strange portents,
Of some great deed seemed near.
The golden corn was bending
Upon its fragile stalk,
While farmers, heedless of their fields,
Paced up and down in talk.

The men seemed stern and altered,
With looks cast on the ground;
With anxious faces, one by one,
The women gathered round;
All talk of flax, or spinning,
Or work, was put away;
The very children seemed afraid
To go alone to play.

One day, out in the meadow
With strangers from the town,
Some secret plan discussing,
The men walked up and down.
Yet, now and then seemed watching,
A strange uncertain gleam,
That looked like lances 'mid the trees,
That stood below the stream.

At eve they all assembled,

Then care and doubt were fled;
With jovial laugh they feasted;
The board was nobly spread.
The elder of the village
Rose up, his glass in hand,
And cried, "We drink the downfall
"Of an accursed land!

"The night is growing darker,
"Ere one more day is flown,
"Bregenz, our foemen's stronghold,
"Bregenz shall be our own!"
The women shrank in terror,
(Yet Pride, too, had her part,)
But one poor Tyrol maiden
Felt death within her heart.

Before her, stood fair Bregenz;
Once more her towers arose;
What were the friends beside her?
Only her country's foes!
The faces of her kinsfolk,
The days of childhood flown,
The echoes of her mountains,
Reclaimed her as their own!

Nothing she heard around her,
(Though shouts rang forth again,)
Gone were the green Swiss valleys,
The pasture, and the plain;
Before her eyes one vision,
And in her heart one cry,
That said, "Go forth, save Bregenz,
And then, if need be, die!"

With trembling haste and breathless,
With noiseless step she sped;
Horses and weary cattle
Were standing in the shed;
She loosed the strong white charger,
That fed from out her hand,
She mounted, and she turned his head
Towards her native land.

Out, out into the darkness
Faster, and still more fast;
The smooth grass flies behind her,
The chestnut wood is past;
She looks up; clouds are heavy:
Why is her steed so slow?
Scarcely the wind beside them,

Can pass them as they go.

"Faster!" she cries, "Oh faster!"
Eleven the church-bells chime:
"Oh God," she cries, "help Bregenz,
And bring me there in time!"
But louder than bells' ringing,
Or lowing of the kine,
Grows nearer in the midnight
The rushing of the Rhine.

Shall not the roaring waters
Their headlong gallop check?
The steed draws back in terror,
She leans upon his neck
To watch the flowing darkness;
The bank is high and steep;
One pause, he staggers forward,
And plunges in the deep.

She strives to pierce the blackness,
And looser throws the rein;
Her steed must breast the waters
That dash above his mane.
How gallantly, how nobly,
He struggles through the foam,
And see, in the far distance,
Shine out the lights of home!

Up the steep banks he bears her,
And now, they rush again
Towards the heights of Bregenz,
That tower above the plain.
They reach the gate of Bregenz,
Just as the midnight rings,
And out come serf and soldier
To meet the news she brings.

Bregenz is saved! Ere daylight
Her battlements are manned;
Defiance greets the army
That marches on the land.
And if to deeds heroic
Should endless fame be paid,
Bregenz does well to honour
The noble Tyrol maid.

Three hundred years are vanished,
And yet upon the hill
An old stone gateway rises,
To do her honour still.

And there, when Bregenz women
Sit spinning in the shade,
They see in quaint old carving
The Charger and the Maid.

And when, to guard old Bregenz,
By gateway, street, and tower,
The warder paces all night long,
And calls each passing hour;
"Nine," "ten," "eleven," he cries aloud,
And then (Oh crown of Fame!)
When midnight pauses in the skies,
He calls the maiden's name!

A FAREWELL

Farewell, oh dream of mine!
I dare not stay;
The hour is come, and time
Will not delay:
Pleasant and dear to me
Wilt thou remain;
No future hour
Brings thee again.

She stands, the Future dim,
And draws me on,
And shows me dearer joys
But thou art gone!
Treasures and Hopes more fair,
Bears she for me,
And yet I linger,
Oh dream, with thee!

Other and brighter days,
Perhaps she brings;
Deeper and holier songs,
Perchance she sings;
But thou and I, fair time,
We too must sever
Oh dream of mine,
Farewell forever!

SOWING AND REAPING

Sow with a generous hand;
Pause not for toil or pain;

Weary not through the heat of summer,
Weary not through the cold spring rain;
But wait till the autumn comes
For the sheaves of golden grain.

Scatter the seed, and fear not,
A table will be spread;
What matter if you are too weary
To eat your hard-earned bread:
Sow, while the earth is broken,
For the hungry must be fed.

Sow; while the seeds are lying
In the warm earth's bosom deep,
And your warm tears fall upon it
They will stir in their quiet sleep;
And the green blades rise the quicker,
Perchance, for the tears you weep.

Then sow; for the hours are fleeting,
And the seed must fall to-day;
And care not what hands shall reap it,
Or if you shall have passed away
Before the waving corn-fields
Shall gladden the sunny day.

Sow; and look onward, upward,
Where the starry light appears
Where, in spite of the coward's doubting,
Or your own heart's trembling fears,
You shall reap in joy the harvest
You have sown to-day in tears.

THE STORM

The tempest rages wild and high,
The waves lift up their voice and cry
Fierce answers to the angry sky,
Miserere Domine.

Through the black night and driving rain,
A ship is struggling, all in vain
To live upon the stormy main;
Miserere Domine.

The thunders roar, the lightnings glare,
Vain is it now to strive or dare;
A cry goes up of great despair,
Miserere Domine.

The stormy voices of the main,
The moaning wind, and pelting rain
Beat on the nursery window pane:—
Miserere Domine.

Warm curtained was the little bed,
Soft pillowed was the little head;
"The storm will wake the child," they said:—
Miserere Domine.

Cowering among his pillows white
He prays, his blue eyes dim with fright,
"Father, save those at sea to-night!"
Miserere Domine.

The morning shone all clear and gay,
On a ship at anchor in the bay,
And on a little child at play,
Gloria tibi Domine!

WORDS

Words are lighter than the cloud-foam
Of the restless ocean spray;
Vainer than the trembling shadow
That the next hour steals away.
By the fall of summer raindrops
Is the air as deeply stirred;
And the rose-leaf that we tread on
Will outlive a word.

Yet, on the dull silence breaking
With a lightning flash, a Word,
Bearing endless desolation
On its blighting wings, I heard:
Earth can forge no keener weapon,
Dealing surer death and pain,
And the cruel echo answered
Through long years again.

I have known one word hang starlike
O'er a dreary waste of years,
And it only shone the brighter
Looked at through a mist of tears;
While a weary wanderer gathered
Hope and heart on Life's dark way,
By its faithful promise, shining
Clearer day by day.

I have known a spirit, calmer
Than the calmest lake, and clear
As the heavens that gazed upon it,
With no wave of hope or fear;
But a storm had swept across it,
And its deepest depths were stirred,
(Never, never more to slumber,)
Only by a word.

I have known a word more gentle
Than the breath of summer air;
In a listening heart it nestled,
And it lived for ever there.
Not the beating of its prison
Stirred it ever, night or day;
Only with the heart's last throbbing
Could it fade away.

Words are mighty, words are living:
Serpents with their venomous stings,
Or bright angels, crowding round us,
With heaven's light upon their wings:
Every word has its own spirit,
True or false, that never dies;
Every word man's lips have uttered
Echoes in God's skies.

A LOVE TOKEN

Do you grieve no costly offering
To the Lady you can make?
One there is, and gifts less worthy
Queens have stooped to take.

Take a Heart of virgin silver,
Fashion it with heavy blows,
Cast it into Love's hot furnace
When it fiercest glows.

With Pain's sharpest point transfix it,
And then carve in letters fair,
Tender dreams and quaint devices,
Fancies sweet and rare.

Set within it Hope's blue sapphire,
Many-changing opal fears,
Blood-red ruby-stones of daring,
Mixed with pearly tears.

And when you have wrought and laboured
Till the gift is all complete,
You may humbly lay your offering
At the Lady's feet.

Should her mood perchance be gracious
With disdainful smiling pride,
She will place it with the trinkets
Glittering at her side.

A TRYST WITH DEATH

I am footsore and very weary,
But I travel to meet a Friend:
The way is long and dreary,
But I know that it soon must end.

He is travelling fast like the whirlwind,
And though I creep slowly on,
We are drawing nearer, nearer,
And the journey is almost done.

Through the heat of many summers,
Through many a springtime rain,
Through long autumns and weary winters,
I have hoped to meet him, in vain.

I know that he will not fail me,
So I count every hour chime,
Every throb of my own heart's beating,
That tells of the flight of Time.

On the day of my birth he plighted
His kingly word to me:—
I have seen him in dreams so often,
That I know what his smile must be.

I have toiled through the sunny woodland,
Through fields that basked in the light;
And through the lone paths in the forest
I crept in the dead of night.

I will not fear at his coming,
Although I must meet him alone;
He will look in my eyes so gently,
And take my hand in his own.

Like a dream all my toil will vanish,

When I lay my head on his breast
But the journey is very weary,
And he only can give me rest!

FIDELIS

You have taken back the promise
That you spoke so long ago;
Taken back the heart you gave me
I must even let it go.
Where Love once has breathed, Pride dieth:
So I struggled, but in vain,
First to keep the links together,
Then to piece the broken chain.

But it might not be, so freely
All your friendship I restore,
And the heart that I had taken
As my own for evermore.
No shade of reproach shall touch you,
Dread no more a claim from me
But I will not have you fancy
That I count myself as free.

I am bound by the old promise;
What can break that golden chain?
Not even the words that you have spoken,
Or the sharpness of my pain:
Do you think, because you fail me
And draw back your hand to-day,
That from out the heart I gave you
My strong love can fade away?

It will live. No eyes may see it;
In my soul it will lie deep,
Hidden from all; but I shall feel it
Often stirring in its sleep.
So remember, that the friendship
Which you now think poor and vain,
Will endure in hope and patience,
Till you ask for it again.

Perhaps in some long twilight hour,
Like those we have known of old,
When past shadows gather round you,
And your present friends grow cold,
You may stretch your hands out towards me,
Ah! you will, I know not when
I shall nurse my love and keep it

Faithfully, for you, till then.

A SHADOW

What lack the valleys and mountains
That once were green and gay?
What lack the babbling fountains?
Their voice is sad to-day.
Only the sound of a voice,
Tender and sweet and low,
That made the earth rejoice,
A year ago!

What lack the tender flowers?
A shadow is on the sun:
What lack the merry hours,
That I long that they were done?
Only two smiling eyes,
That told of joy and mirth:
They are shining in the skies,
I mourn on earth!

What lacks my heart, that makes it
So weary and full of pain,
That trembling Hope forsakes it,
Never to come again?
Only another heart,
Tender and all mine own,
In the still grave it lies;
I weep alone!

THE SAILOR BOY

My Life you ask of? why, you know
Full soon my little Life is told;
It has had no great joy or woe,
For I am only twelve years old.
Ere long I hope I shall have been
On my first voyage, and wonders seen.
Some princess I may help to free
From pirates, on a far-off sea;
Or, on some desert isle be left,
Of friends and shipmates all bereft.

For the first time I venture forth,
From our blue mountains of the north.
My kinsman kept the lodge that stood

Guarding the entrance near the wood,
By the stone gateway grey and old,
With quaint devices carved about,
And broken shields; while dragons bold
Glared on the common world without;
And the long trembling ivy spray
Half hid the centuries' decay.
In solitude and silence grand
The castle towered above the land:
The castle of the Earl, whose name
(Wrapped in old bloody legends) came
Down through the times when Truth and Right
Bent down to armed Pride and Might.
He owned the country far and near;
And, for some weeks in every year,
(When the brown leaves were falling fast
And the long, lingering autumn passed,)
He would come down to hunt the deer,
With hound and horse in splendid pride.
The story lasts the live-long year,
The peasant's winter evening fills,
When he is gone and they abide
In the lone quiet of their hills.

I longed, too, for the happy night,
When, all with torches flaring bright,
The crowding villagers would stand,
A patient, eager, waiting band,
Until the signal ran like flame
"They come!" and, slackening speed, they came.
Outriders first, in pomp and state,
Pranced on their horses through the gate;
Then the four steeds as black as night,
All decked with trappings blue and white,
Drew through the crowd that opened wide,
The Earl and Countess side by side.
The stern grave Earl, with formal smile
And glistening eyes and stately pride,
Could ne'er my childish gaze beguile
From the fair presence by his side.
The lady's soft sad glance, her eyes,
(Like stars that shone in summer skies,)
Her pure white face so calmly bent,
With gentle greetings round her sent
Her look, that always seemed to gaze
Where the blue past had closed again
Over some happy shipwrecked days,
With all their freight of love and pain:
She did not even seem to see
The little lord upon her knee.
And yet he was like angel fair,

With rosy cheeks and golden hair,
That fell on shoulders white as snow:
But the blue eyes that shone below
His clustering rings of auburn curls,
Were not his mother's, but the Earl's.

I feared the Earl, so cold and grim,
I never dared be seen by him.
When through our gate he used to ride,
My kinsman Walter bade me hide;
He said he was so stern.
So, when the hunt came past our way,
I always hastened to obey,
Until I heard the bugles play
The notes of their return.
But she, my very heart-strings stir
Whene'er I speak or think of her
The whole wide world could never see
A noble lady such as she,
So full of angel charity.

Strange things of her our neighbours told
In the long winter evenings cold,
Around the fire. They would draw near
And speak half-whispering, as in fear;
As if they thought the Earl could hear
Their treason 'gainst his name.
They thought the story that his pride
Had stooped to wed a low-born bride,
A stain upon his fame.
Some said 'twas false; there could not be
Such blot on his nobility:
But others vowed that they had heard
The actual story word for word,
From one who well my lady knew,
And had declared the story true.

In a far village, little known,
She dwelt, so ran the tale, alone.
A widowed bride, yet, oh! so bright,
Shone through the mist of grief, her charms;
They said it was the loveliest sight
She with her baby in her arms.
The Earl, one summer morning, rode
By the sea-shore where she abode;
Again he came, that vision sweet
Drew him reluctant to her feet.
Fierce must the struggle in his heart
Have been, between his love and pride,
Until he chose that wondrous part,
To ask her to become his bride.

Yet, ere his noble name she bore,
He made her vow that nevermore
She would behold her child again,
But hide his name and hers from men.
The trembling promise duly spoken,
All links of the low past were broken;
And she arose to take her stand
Amid the nobles of the land.
Then all would wonder, could it be
That one so lowly born as she,
Raised to such height of bliss, should seem
Still living in some weary dream?
'Tis true she bore with calmest grace
The honours of her lofty place,
Yet never smiled, in peace or joy,
Not even to greet her princely boy.
She heard, with face of white despair,
The cannon thunder through the air,
That she had given the Earl an heir.
Nay, even more, (they whispered low,
As if they scarce durst fancy so,)
That, through her lofty wedded life,
No word, no tone, betrayed the wife.
Her look seemed ever in the past;
Never to him it grew more sweet;
The self-same weary glance she cast
Upon the grey-hound at her feet,
As upon him, who bade her claim
The crowning honour of his name.

This gossip, if old Walter heard,
He checked it with a scornful word:
I never durst such tales repeat;
He was too serious and discreet
To speak of what his lord might do;
Besides, he loved my lady too.
And many a time, I recollect,
They were together in the wood;
He, with an air of grave respect,
And earnest look, uncovered stood.
And though their speech I never heard,
(Save now and then a louder word,)
I saw he spake as none but one
She loved and trusted, durst have done;
For oft I watched them in the shade
That the close forest branches made,
Till slanting golden sunbeams came
And smote the fir-trees into flame,
A radiant glory round her lit,
Then down her white robes seemed to flit,
Gilding the brown leaves on the ground,

And all the waving ferns around.
While by some gloomy pine she leant
And he in earnest talk would stand,
I saw the tear-drops, as she bent,
Fall on the flowers in her hand.
Strange as it seemed and seems to be,
That one so sad, so cold as she,
Could love a little child like me
Yet so it was. I never heard
Such tender words as she would say,
And murmurs, sweeter than a word,
Would breathe upon me as I lay.
While I, in smiling joy, would rest,
For hours, my head upon her breast.
Our neighbours said that none could see
In me the common childish charms,
(So grave and still I used to be,)
And yet she held me in her arms,
In a fond clasp, so close, so tight
I often dream of it at night.
She bade me tell her all, no other
My childish thoughts e'er cared to know:
For I, I never knew my mother;
I was an orphan long ago.
And I could all my fancies pour,
That gentle loving face before.
She liked to hear me tell her all;
How that day I had climbed the tree,
To make the largest fir-cones fall;
And how one day I hoped to be
A sailor on the deep blue sea
She loved to hear it all!

Then wondrous things she used to tell,
Of the strange dreams that she had known.
I used to love to hear them well,
If only for her sweet low tone,
Sometimes so sad, although I knew
That such things never could be true.
One day she told me such a tale
It made me grow all cold and pale,
The fearful thing she told!
Of a poor woman mad and wild
Who coined the life-blood of her child,
And tempted by a fiend, had sold
The heart out of her breast for gold.
But, when she saw me frightened seem,
She smiled, and said it was a dream.
When I look back and think of her,
My very heart-strings seem to stir;
How kind, how fair she was, how good

I cannot tell you. If I could
You, too, would love her. The mere thought
Of her great love for me has brought
Tears in my eyes: though far away,
It seems as it were yesterday.
And just as when I look on high
Through the blue silence of the sky,
Fresh stars shine out, and more and more,
Where I could see so few before;
So, the more steadily I gaze
Upon those far-off misty days,
Fresh words, fresh tones, fresh memories start
Before my eyes and in my heart.
I can remember how one day
(Talking in silly childish way)
I said how happy I should be
If I were like her son, as fair,
With just such bright blue eyes as he,
And such long locks of golden hair.
A strange smile on her pale face broke,
And in strange solemn words she spoke:
"My own, my darling one, no, no!
I love you, far, far better so.
I would not change the look you bear,
Or one wave of your dark brown hair.
The mere glance of your sunny eyes,
Deep in my deepest soul I prize
Above that baby fair!
Not one of all the Earl's proud line
In beauty ever matched with thine;
And, 'tis by thy dark locks thou art
Bound even faster round my heart,
And made more wholly mine!"
And then she paused, and weeping said,
"You are like one who now is dead
Who sleeps in a far-distant grave.
Oh may God grant that you may be
As noble and as good as he,
As gentle and as brave!"
Then in my childish way I cried,
"The one you tell me of who died,
Was he as noble as the Earl?"
I see her red lips scornful curl,
I feel her hold my hand again
So tightly, that I shrink in pain
I seem to hear her say,
"He whom I tell you of, who died,
He was so noble and so gay,
So generous and so brave,
That the proud Earl by his dear side
Would look a craven slave."

She paused; then, with a quivering sigh,
She laid her hand upon my brow:
"Live like him, darling, and so die.
Remember that he tells you now,
True peace, real honour, and content,
In cheerful pious toil abide;
That gold and splendour are but sent
To curse our vanity and pride."
One day some childish fever pain
Burnt in my veins and fired my brain.
Moaning, I turned from side to side;
And, sobbing in my bed, I cried,
Till night in calm and darkness crept
Around me, and at last I slept.
When suddenly I woke to see
The Lady bending over me.
The drops of cold November rain
Were falling from her long, damp hair;
Her anxious eyes were dim with pain;
Yet she looked wondrous fair.
Arrayed for some great feast she came,
With stones that shone and burnt like flame;
Wound round her neck, like some bright snake,
And set like stars within her hair,
They sparkled so, they seemed to make
A glory everywhere.
I felt her tears upon my face,
Her kisses on my eyes;
And a strange thought I could not trace
I felt within my heart arise;
And, half in feverish pain, I said:
"Oh if my mother were not dead!"
And Walter bade me sleep; but she
Said, "Is it not the same to thee
That I watch by thy bed?"
I answered her, "I love you, too;
But it can never be the same;
She was no Countess like to you,
Nor wore such sparkling stones of flame."
Oh the wild look of fear and dread!
The cry she gave of bitter woe!
I often wonder what I said
To make her moan and shudder so.
Through the long night she tended me
With such sweet care and charity.
But should weary you to tell
All that I know and love so well:
Yet one night more stands out alone
With a sad sweetness all its own.

The wind blew loud that dreary night:

Its wailing voice I well remember:
The stars shone out so large and bright
Upon the frosty fir-boughs white,
That dreary night of cold December.
I saw old Walter silent stand,
Watching the soft white flakes of snow
With looks I could not understand,
Of strange perplexity and woe.
At last he turned and took my hand,
And said the Countess just had sent
To bid us come; for she would fain
See me once more, before she went
Away, never to come again.
We came in silence through the wood
(Our footfall was the only sound)
To where the great white castle stood,
With darkness shadowing it around.
Breathless, we trod with cautious care
Up the great echoing marble stair;
Trembling, by Walter's hand I held,
Scared by the splendours I beheld:
Now thinking, "Should the Earl appear!"
Now looking up with giddy fear
To the dim vaulted roof, that spread
Its gloomy arches overhead.
Long corridors we softly past,
(My heart was beating loud and fast)
And reached the Lady's room at last:
A strange faint odour seemed to weigh
Upon the dim and darkened air;
One shaded lamp, with softened ray,
Scarce showed the gloomy splendour there.
The dull red brands were burning low,
And yet a fitful gleam of light,
Would now and then, with sudden glow,
Start forth, then sink again in night.
I gazed around, yet half in fear,
Till Walter told me to draw near:
And in the strange and flickering light,
Towards the Lady's bed I crept;
All folded round with snowy white,
She lay; (one would have said she slept;)
So still the look of that white face,
It seemed as it were carved in stone,
I paused before I dared to place
Within her cold white hand my own.
But, with a smile of sweet surprise,
She turned to me her dreamy eyes;
And slowly, as if life were pain,
She drew me in her arms to lie:
She strove to speak, and strove in vain;

Each breath was like a long-drawn sigh.
The throbs that seemed to shake her breast,
The trembling clasp, so loose and weak,
At last grew calmer, and at rest;
And then she strove once more to speak:
"My God, I thank thee, that my pain
Of day by day and year by year,
Has not been suffered all in vain,
And I may die while he is near.
I will not fear but that Thy grace
Has swept away my sin and woe,
And sent this little angel face,
In my last hour to tell me so."
(And here her voice grew faint and low,)
"My child, where'er thy life may go,
To know that thou art brave and true,
Will pierce the highest heavens through,
And even there my soul shall be
More joyful for this thought of thee."
She folded her white hands, and stayed;
All cold and silently she lay:
I knelt beside the bed, and prayed
The prayer she used to make me say.
I said it many times, and then
She did not move, but seemed to be
In a deep sleep, nor stirred again.
No sound woke in the silent room,
Or broke the dim and solemn gloom,
Save when the brands that burnt so low,
With noisy fitful gleam of light,
Would spread around a sudden glow,
Then sink in silence and in night.
How long I stood I do not know:
At last poor Walter came, and said
(So sadly) that we now must go,
And whispered, she we loved was dead.
He bade me kiss her face once more,
Then led me sobbing to the door.
I scarcely knew what dying meant,
Yet a strange grief, before unknown,
Weighed on my spirit as we went
And left her lying all alone.

We went to the far North once more,
To seek the well-remembered home,
Where my poor kinsman dwelt before,
Whence now he was too old to roam;
And there six happy years we past,
Happy and peaceful till the last;
When poor old Walter died, and he
Blessed me and said I now might be

A sailor on the deep blue sea.
And so I go; and yet in spite
Of all the joys I long to know,
Though I look onward with delight,
With something of regret I go;
And young or old, on land or sea,
One guiding memory I shall take
Of what She prayed that I might be,
And what I will be for her sake!

A CROWN OF SORROW

A Sorrow, wet with early tears
Yet bitter, had been long with me;
I wearied of this weight of years,
And would be free.

I tore my Sorrow from my heart,
I cast it far away in scorn;
Right joyful that we two could part
Yet most forlorn.

I sought, (to take my Sorrow's place,)
Over the world for flower or gem
But she had had an ancient grace
Unknown to them.

I took once more with strange delight
My slighted Sorrow; proudly now,
I wear it, set with stars of light,
Upon my brow.

THE LESSON OF THE WAR (1855)

The feast is spread through England
For rich and poor to-day;
Greetings and laughter may be there,
But thoughts are far away;
Over the stormy ocean,
Over the dreary track,
Where some are gone, whom England
Will never welcome back.

Breathless she waits, and listens
For every eastern breeze
That bears upon its bloody wings
News from beyond the seas.

The leafless branches stirring
Make many a watcher start;
The distant tramp of steed may send
A throb from heart to heart.

The rulers of the nation,
The poor ones at their gate,
With the same eager wonder
The same great news await.
The poor man's stay and comfort,
The rich man's joy and pride,
Upon the bleak Crimean shore
Are fighting side by side.

The bullet comes and either
A desolate hearth may see;
And God alone to-night knows where
The vacant place may be!
The dread that stirs the peasant
Thrills nobles' hearts with fear
Yet above selfish sorrow
Both hold their country dear.

The rich man who reposes
In his ancestral shade,
The peasant at his ploughshare,
The worker at his trade,
Each one his all his perilled,
Each has the same great stake,
Each soul can but have patience,
Each heart can only break!

Hushed is all party clamour;
One thought in every heart,
One dread in every household,
Has bid such strife depart.
England has called her children;
Long silent, the word came
That lit the smouldering ashes
Through all the land to flame.

Oh you who toil and suffer,
You gladly heard the call;
But those you sometimes envy
Have they not given their all?
Oh you who rule the nation,
Take now the toil-worn hand
Brothers you are in sorrow,
In duty to your land.
Learn but this noble lesson
Ere Peace returns again,

And the life-blood of Old England
Will not be shed in vain.

THE TWO SPIRITS (1855)

Last night, when weary silence fell on all,
And starless skies arose so dim and vast,
I heard the Spirit of the Present call
Upon the sleeping Spirit of the Past.
Far off and near, I saw their radiance shine,
And listened while they spoke of deeds divine.

The Spirit of the Past.

My deeds are writ in iron;
My glory stands alone;
A veil of shadowy honour
Upon my tombs is thrown;
The great names of my heroes
Like gems in history lie;
To live they deemed ignoble,
Had they the chance to die!

The Spirit of the Present.

My children, too, are honoured;
Dear shall their memory be
To the proud lands that own them;
Dearer than thine to thee;
For, though they hold that sacred
Is God's great gift of life,
At the first call of duty
They rush into the strife!

The Spirit of the Past.

Then, with all valiant precepts
Woman's soft heart was fraught;
"Death, not dishonour," echoed
The war-cry she had taught.
Fearless and glad, those mothers,
At bloody deaths elate,
Cried out they bore their children
Only for such a fate!

The Spirit of the Present.

Though such stern laws of honour
Are faded now away,

Yet many a mourning mother,
With nobler grief than they,
Bows down in sad submission:
The heroes of the fight
Learnt at her knee the lesson,
"For God and for the Right!"

The Spirit of the Past.

No voice there spake of sorrow:
They saw the noblest fall
With no repining murmur;
Stern Fate was lord of all.
And when the loved ones perished,
One cry alone arose,
Waking the startled echoes,
"Vengeance upon our foes!"

The Spirit of the Present.

Grief dwells in France and England
For many a noble son;
Yet louder than the sorrow,
"Thy will, Oh God, be done!"
From desolate homes is rising
One prayer, "Let carnage cease!
On friends and foes have mercy,
Oh Lord, and give us peace!"

The Spirit of the Past.

Then, every hearth was honoured
That sent its children forth,
To spread their country's glory,
And gain her south or north.
Then, little recked they numbers,
No band would ever fly,
But stern and resolute they stood
To conquer or to die.

The Spirit of the Present.

And now from France and England
Their dearest and their best
Go forth to succour freedom,
To help the much oppressed;
Now, let the far-off Future
And Past bow down to-day,
Before the few young hearts that hold
Whole armaments at bay.

The Spirit of the Past.

Then, each one strove for honour,
Each for a deathless name;
Love, home, rest, joy, were offered
As sacrifice to Fame.
They longed that in far ages
Their deeds might still be told,
And distant times and nations
Their names in honour hold.

The Spirit of the Present.

Though nursed by such old legends,
Our heroes of to-day
Go cheerfully to battle
As children go to play;
They gaze with awe and wonder
On your great names of pride,
Unconscious that their own will shine
In glory side by side!

Day dawned; and as the Spirits passed away,
Methought I saw, in the dim morning grey,
The Past's bright diadem had paled before
The starry crown the glorious Present wore.

A LITTLE LONGER

A little longer yet, a little longer,
Shall violets bloom for thee, and sweet birds sing;
And the lime branches where soft winds are blowing,
Shall murmur the sweet promise of the Spring!

A little longer yet, a little longer,
Thou shalt behold the quiet of the morn;
While tender grasses and awakening flowers
Send up a golden mist to greet the dawn!

A little longer yet, a little longer,
The tenderness of twilight shall be thine,
The rosy clouds that float o'er dying daylight,
Nor fade till trembling stars begin to shine.

A little longer yet, a little longer,
Shall starry night be beautiful for thee;
And the cold moon shall look through the blue silence,
Flooding her silver path upon the sea.

A little longer yet, a little longer,
Life shall be thine; life with its power to will;
Life with its strength to bear, to love, to conquer,
Bringing its thousand joys thy heart to fill.

A little longer yet, a little longer,
The voices thou hast loved shall charm thine ear;
And thy true heart, that now beats quick to hear them,
A little longer yet shall hold them dear.

A little longer yet, joy while thou mayest;
Love and rejoice! for time has nought in store;
And soon the darkness of the grave shall bid thee
Love and rejoice and feel and know no more.

A little longer still, Patience, Beloved:
A little longer still, ere Heaven unroll
The Glory, and the Brightness, and the Wonder,
Eternal, and divine, that waits thy Soul!

A little longer ere Life true, immortal,
(Not this our shadowy Life,) will be thine own;
And thou shalt stand where winged Archangels worship,
And trembling bow before the Great White Throne.

A little longer still, and Heaven awaits thee,
And fills thy spirit with a great delight;
Then our pale joys will seem a dream forgotten,
Our Sun a darkness, and our Day a Night.

A little longer, and thy Heart, Beloved,
Shall beat for ever with a Love divine;
And joy so pure, so mighty, so eternal,
No creature knows and lives, will then be thine.

A little longer yet, and angel voices
Shall ring in heavenly chant upon thine ear;
Angels and Saints await thee, and God needs thee:
Beloved, can we bid thee linger here!

GRIEF

An ancient enemy have I,
And either he or I must die;
For he never leaveth me,
Never gives my soul relief,
Never lets my sorrow cease,
Never gives my spirit peace
For mine enemy is Grief!

Pale he is, and sad and stern;
And whene'er he cometh nigh,
Blue and dim the torches burn,
Pale and shrunk the roses turn;
While my heart that he has pierced
Many a time with fiery lance,
Beats and trembles at his glance:
Clad in burning steel is he,
All my strength he can defy;
For he never leaveth me
And one of us must die!

I have said, "Let ancient sages
Charm me from my thoughts of pain!"
So I read their deepest pages,
And I strove to think in vain!
Wisdom's cold calm words I tried,
But he was seated by my side:—
Learning I have won in vain;
She cannot rid me of my pain.

When at last soft sleep comes o'er me,
A cold hand is on my heart;
Stern sad eyes are there before me;
Not in dreams will he depart:
And when the same dreary vision
From my weary brain has fled,
Daylight brings the living phantom,
He is seated by my bed,
Bending o'er me all the while,
With his cruel, bitter smile,
Ever with me, ever nigh;
And either he or I must die!

Then I said, long time ago,
"I will flee to other climes,
I will leave mine ancient foe!"
Though I wandered far and wide
Still he followed at my side.

And I fled where the blue waters
Bathe the sunny isles of Greece;
Where Thessalian mountains rise
Up against the purple skies;
Where a haunting memory liveth
In each wood and cave and rill;
But no dream of gods could help me
He went with me still!

I have been where Nile's broad river

Flows upon the burning sand;
Where the desert monster broodeth,
Where the Eastern palm-trees stand;
I have been where pathless forests
Spread a black eternal shade;
Where the lurking panther hiding
Glares from every tangled glade;
But in vain I wandered wide,
He was always by my side!
Then I fled where snows eternal
Cold and dreary ever lie;
Where the rosy lightnings gleam,
Flashing through the northern sky;
Where the red sun turns again
Back upon his path of pain;
But a shadowy form was with me
I had fled in vain!

I have thought, "If I can gaze
Sternly on him he will fade,
For I know that he is nothing
But a dim ideal shade."
As I gazed at him the more,
He grew stronger than before!

Then I said, "Mine arm is strong,
I will make him turn and flee:"
I have struggled with him long
But that could never be!

Once I battled with him so
That I thought I laid him low;
Then in trembling joy I fled,
While again and still again
Murmuring to myself I said,
"Mine old enemy is dead!"
And I stood beneath the stars,
When a chill came on my frame,
And a fear I could not name,
And a sense of quick despair,
And, lo! mine enemy was there!

Listen, for my soul is weary,
Weary of its endless woe;
I have called on one to aid me
Mightier even than my foe.
Strength and hope fail day by day;
I shall cheat him of his prey;
Someday soon, I know not when,
He will stab me through and through;
He has wounded me before,

But my heart can bear no more;
Pray that hour may come to me,
Only then shall I be free;
Death alone has strength to take me
Where my foe can never be;
Death, and Death alone, has power
To conquer mine old enemy!

THE TRIUMPH OF TIME

The tender delicate Flowers,
I saw them fanned by a warm western wind,
Fed by soft summer showers,
Shielded by care, and yet, (oh Fate unkind!)
Fade in a few short hours.

The gentle and the gay,
Rich in a glorious Future of bright deeds,
Rejoicing in the day,
Are met by Death, who sternly, sadly leads
Them far away.

And Hopes, perfumed and bright,
So lately shining, wet with dew and tears,
Trembling in morning light;
I saw them change to dark and anxious fears
Before the night!

I wept that all must die
"Yet Love," I cried, "doth live, and conquer death"
And Time passed by,
And breathed on Love, and killed it with his breath
Ere Death was nigh.

More bitter far than all
It was to know that Love could change and die
Hush! for the ages call
"The Love of God lives through eternity,
And conquers all!"

A PARTING

Without one bitter feeling let us part
And for the years in which your love has shed
A radiance like a glory round my head,
I thank you, yes, I thank you from my heart.

I thank you for the cherished hope of years,
A starry future, dim and yet divine,
Winging its way from Heaven to be mine,
Laden with joy, and ignorant of tears.

I thank you, yes, I thank you even more
That my heart learnt not without love to live,
But gave and gave, and still had more to give,
From an abundant and exhaustless store.

I thank you, and no grief is in these tears;
I thank you, not in bitterness but truth,
For the fair vision that adorned my youth
And glorified so many happy years.

Yet how much more I thank you that you tore
At length the veil your hand had woven away,
Which hid my idol was a thing of clay,
And false the altar I had knelt before.

I thank you that you taught me the stern truth,
(None other could have told and I believed,)
That vain had been my life, and I deceived,
And wasted all the purpose of my youth.

I thank you that your hand dashed down the shrine,
Wherein my idol worship I had paid;
Else had I never known a soul was made
To serve and worship only the Divine.

I thank you that the heart I cast away
On such as you, though broken, bruised and crushed,
Now that its fiery throbbing is all hushed,
Upon a worthier altar I can lay.

I thank you for the lesson that such love
Is a perverting of God's royal right,
That it is made but for the Infinite,
And all too great to live except above.

I thank you for a terrible awaking,
And if reproach seemed hidden in my pain,
And sorrow seemed to cry on your disdain,
Know that my blessing lay in your forsaking.

Farewell for ever now:—in peace we part;
And should an idle vision of my tears
Arise before your soul in after years
Remember that I thank you from my heart!

THE GOLDEN GATE

Dim shadows gather thickly round, and up the misty stair they climb,
The cloudy stair that upward leads to where the closed portals shine,
Round which the kneeling spirits wait the opening of the Golden Gate.

And some with eager longing go, still pressing forward, hand in hand,
And some with weary step and slow, look back where their Beloved stand
Yet up the misty stair they climb, led onward by the Angel Time.

As unseen hands roll back the doors, the light that floods the very air
Is but the shadow from within, of the great glory hidden there
And morn and eve, and soon and late, the shadows pass within the gate.

As one by one they enter in, and the stern portals close once more,
The halo seems to linger round those kneeling closest to the door:
The joy that lightened from that place shines still upon the watcher's face.

The faint low echo that we hear of far-off music seems to fill
The silent air with love and fear, and the world's clamours all grow still,
Until the portals close again, and leave us toiling on in pain.

Complain not that the way is long, what road is weary that leads there?
But let the Angel take thy hand, and lead thee up the misty stair,
And then with beating heart await, the opening of the Golden Gate.

PHANTOMS

Back, ye Phantoms of the Past;
In your dreary caves remain:
What have I to do with memories
Of a long-forgotten pain?

For my Present is all peaceful,
And my Future nobly planned:
Long ago Time's mighty billows
Swept your footsteps from the sand.

Back into your caves; nor haunt me
With your voices full of woe;
I have buried grief and sorrow
In the depths of Long-ago.

See the glorious clouds of morning
Roll away, and clear and bright
Shine the rays of cloudless daylight
Wherefore will ye moan of night?

Never shall my heart be burthened
With its ancient woe and fears;
I can drive them from my presence,
I can check these foolish tears.

Back, ye Phantoms; leave, oh leave me
To a new and happy lot;
Speak no more of things departed;
Leave me for I know ye not.

Can it be that 'mid my gladness
I must ever hear you wail,
Of the grief that wrung my spirit,
And that made my cheek so pale?

Joy is mine; but your sad voices
Murmur ever in mine ear:
Vain is all the Future's promise,
While the dreary Past is here.

Vain, oh worse than vain, the Visions
That my heart, my life would fill,
If the Past's relentless phantoms
Call upon me still!

THANKFULNESS

My God, I thank Thee who hast made
The Earth so bright;
So full of splendour and of joy,
Beauty and light;
So many glorious things are here,
Noble and right!

I thank Thee, too, that Thou hast made
Joy to abound;
So many gentle thoughts and deeds
Circling us round,
That in the darkest spot of Earth
Some love is found.

I thank Thee more that all our joy
Is touched with pain;
That shadows fall on brightest hours;
That thorns remain;
So that Earth's bliss may be our guide,
And not our chain.

For Thou who knowest, Lord, how soon

Our weak heart clings,
Hast given us joys, tender and true,
Yet all with wings,
So that we see, gleaming on high,
Diviner things!

I thank Thee, Lord, that Thou hast kept
The best in store;
We have enough, yet not too much
To long for more:
A yearning for a deeper peace,
Not known before.

I thank Thee, Lord, that here our souls,
Though amply blest,
Can never find, although they seek,
A perfect rest
Nor ever shall, until they lean
On Jesus' breast!

HOME-SICKNESS

Where I am, the halls are gilded,
Stored with pictures bright and rare;
Strains of deep melodious music
Float upon the perfumed air:—
Nothing stirs the dreary silence
Save the melancholy sea,
Near the poor and humble cottage,
Where I fain would be!

Where I am, the sun is shining,
And the purple windows glow,
Till their rich armorial shadows
Stain the marble floor below:—
Faded Autumn leaves are trembling,
On the withered jasmine tree,
Creeping round the little casement,
Where I fain would be!

Where I am, the days are passing
O'er a pathway strewn with flowers;
Song and joy and starry pleasures
Crown the happy smiling hours:—
Slowly, heavily, and sadly,
Time with weary wings must flee,
Marked by pain, and toil, and sorrow,
Where I fain would be!

Where I am, the great and noble
Tell me of renown and fame,
And the red wine sparkles highest,
To do honour to my name:—
Far away a place is vacant,
By a humble hearth, for me,
Dying embers dimly show it,
Where I fain would be!

Where I am, are glorious dreaminess,
Science, genius, art divine;
And the great minds whom all honour
Interchange their thoughts with mine:—
A few simple hearts are waiting,
Longing, wearying, for me,
Far away where tears are falling,
Where I fain would be!

Where I am, all think me happy,
For so well I play my part,
None can guess, who smile around me,
How far distant is my heart
Far away, in a poor cottage,
Listening to the dreary sea,
Where the treasures of my life are,
Where I fain would be!

WISHES

All the fluttering wishes
Caged within thy heart
Beat their wings against it,
Longing to depart,
Till they shake their prison
With their wounded cry;
Open wide thy heart to-day,
And let the captives fly.

Let them first fly upward
Through the starry air,
Till you almost lose them,
For their home is there;
Then, with outspread pinions,
Circling round and round,
Wing their way, wherever
Want and woe are found.

Where the weary stitcher
Toils for daily bread;

Where the lonely watcher
Watches by her dead;
Where with thin weak fingers,
Toiling at the loom,
Stand the little children,
Blighted ere they bloom.

Where, by darkness blinded,
Groping for the light,
With distorted conscience
Men do wrong for right;
Where, in the cold shadow,
By smooth pleasure thrown,
Human hearts by hundreds
Harden into stone.

Where on dusty highways,
With faint heart and slow,
Cursing the glad sunlight,
Hungry outcasts go:
Where all mirth is silenced,
And the hearth is chill,
For one place is empty,
And one voice is still.

Some hearts will be lighter
While your captives roam
For their tender singing,
Then recal them home;
When the sunny hours
Into night depart,
Softly they will nestle
In a quiet heart.

THE PEACE OF GOD

We ask for Peace, oh Lord!
Thy children ask Thy Peace;
Not what the world calls rest,
That toil and care should cease,
That through bright sunny hours
Calm Life should fleet away,
And tranquil night should fade
In smiling day;
It is not for such Peace that we would pray.

We ask for Peace, oh Lord!
Yet not to stand secure,
Girt round with iron Pride,

Contented to endure:
Crushing the gentle strings
That human hearts should know,
Untouched by others' joy
Or others' woe;
Thou, oh dear Lord, wilt never teach us so.

We ask Thy Peace, oh Lord!
Through storm, and fear, and strife,
To light and guide us on,
Through a long struggling life:
While no success or gain
Shall cheer the desperate fight,
Or nerve, what the world calls,
Our wasted might:—
Yet pressing through the darkness to the light.

It is Thine own, oh Lord,
Who toil while others sleep;
Who sow with loving care
What other hands shall reap:
They lean on Thee entranced,
In calm and perfect rest:
Give us that Peace, oh Lord,
Divine and blest,
Thou keepest for those hearts who love Thee best.

LIFE IN DEATH AND DEATH IN LIFE

I

If the dread day that calls thee hence,
Through a red mist of fear should loom,
(Closing in deadliest night and gloom
Long hours of aching dumb suspense,)
And leave me to my lonely doom.

I think, beloved, I could see
In thy dear eyes the loving light
Glaze into vacancy and night,
And still say, "God is good to me,
And all that He decrees is right."

That, watching thy slow struggling breath,
And answering each imperfect sign,
I still could pray thy prayer and mine,
And tell thee, dear, though this was death,
That God was love, and love divine.

Could hold thee in my arms, and lay
Upon my heart thy weary head,
And meet thy last smile ere it fled;
Then hear, as in a dream, one say,
"Now all is over, she is dead."

Could smooth thy garments with fond care,
And cross thy hands upon thy breast,
And kiss thine eyelids down to rest,
And yet say no word of despair,
But, through my sobbing, "It is best."

Could stifle down the gnawing pain,
And say, "We still divide our life,
She has the rest, and I the strife,
And mine the loss, and hers the gain:
My ill with bliss for her is rife."

Then turn, and the old duties take
Alone now, yet with earnest will
Gathering sweet sacred traces still
To help me on, and, for thy sake,
My heart and life and soul to fill.

I think I could check vain weak tears,
And toil, although the world's great space
Held nothing but one vacant place,
And see the dark and weary years
Lit only by a vanished grace.

And sometimes, when the day was o'er,
Call up the tender past again:
Its painful joy, its happy pain,
And live it over yet once more,
And say, "But few more years remain."

And then, when I had striven my best,
And all around would smiling say,
"See how Time makes all grief decay,"
Would lie down thankfully to rest,
And seek thee in eternal day.

II

But if the day should ever rise
It could not and it cannot be
Yet, if the sun should ever see,
Looking upon us from his skies,
A day that took thy heart from me;

If loving thee still more and more,
And still so willing to be blind,
I should the bitter knowledge find,
That Time had eaten out the core
Of love, and left the empty rind;

If the poor lifeless words, at last,
(The soul gone, that was once so sweet,)
Should cease my eager heart to cheat,
And crumble back into the past,
And show the whole a vain deceit;

If I should see thee turn away,
And know that prayer, and time, and pain,
Could no more thy lost love regain,
Than bid the hours of dying day
Gleam in their mid-day noon again;

If I should loose thy hand, and know
That henceforth we must dwell apart,
Since I had seen thy love depart,
And only count the hours flow
By the dull throbbing of my heart;

If I should gaze and gaze in vain
Into thine eyes so deep and clear,
And read the truth of all my fear
Half mixed with pity for my pain,
And sorrow for the vanished year;

If not to grieve thee overmuch,
I strove to counterfeit disdain,
And weave me a new life again,
Which thy life could not mar, or touch,
And so smile down my bitter pain;

The ghost of my dead Past would rise
And mock me, and I could not dare
Look to a future of despair,
Or even to the eternal skies,
For I should still be lonely there.

All Truth, all Honour, then would seem
Vain clouds, which the first wind blew by;
All Trust, a folly doomed to die;
All Life, a useless empty dream;
All Love, since thine had failed a lie.

But see, thy tender smile has cast
My fear away: this thought of mine
Is treason to my Love and thine;

For Love is Life, and Death at last
Crowns it eternal and divine!

RECOLLECTIONS

As strangers, you and I are here;
We both as aliens stand,
Where once, in years gone by, I dwelt
No stranger in the land.
Then while you gaze on park and stream,
Let me remain apart,
And listen to the awakened sound
Of voices in my heart.

Here, where upon the velvet lawn
The cedar spreads its shade,
And by the flower-beds all around,
Bright roses bloom and fade;
Shrill merry childish laughter rings,
And baby voices sweet,
And by me, on the path, I hear
The tread of little feet.

Down the dark avenue of limes,
Whose perfume loads the air,
Whose boughs are rustling overhead,
(For the west wind is there,)
I hear the sound of earnest talk,
Warnings and counsels wise,
And the quick questioning that brought
Such gentle calm replies.

Still the light bridge hangs o'er the lake,
Where broad-leaved lilies lie,
And the cool water shows again
The cloud that moves on high;
And one voice speaks, in tones I thought
The past for ever kept;
But now I know, deep in my heart
Its echoes only slept.

I hear, within the shady porch,
Once more, the measured sound
Of the old ballads that were read,
While we sat listening round;
The starry passion-flower still
Up the green trellice climbs;
The tendrils waving seem to keep
The cadence of the rhymes.

I might have striven, and striven in vain,
Such visions to recall,
Well known and yet forgotten; now
I see, I hear, them all!
The Present pales before the Past,
Who comes with angel wings;
As in a dream I stand, amidst
Strange yet familiar things!

Enough; so let us go, mine eyes
Are blinded by their tears;
A voice speaks to my soul to-day
Of long forgotten years.
And yet the vision in my heart,
In a few hours more,
Will fade into the silent past,
Silently as before.

ILLUSION

Where the golden corn is bending,
And the singing reapers pass,
Where the chestnut woods are sending
Leafy showers upon the grass,

The blue river onward flowing
Mingles with its noisy strife,
The murmur of the flowers growing,
And the hum of insect life.

I, from that rich plain was gazing
Towards the snowy mountains high,
Who their gleaming peaks were raising
Up against the purple sky.

And the glory of their shining,
Bathed in clouds of rosy light,
Set my weary spirit pining
For a home so pure and bright!

So I left the plain, and weary,
Fainting, yet with hope sustained,
Toiled through pathways long and dreary
Till the mountain top was gained.

Lo! the height that I had taken,
As so shining from below,
Was a desolate, forsaken

Region of perpetual snow.

I am faint, my feet are bleeding,
All my feeble strength is worn,
In the plain no soul is heeding,
I am here alone, forlorn.

Lights are shining, bells are tolling,
In the busy vale below;
Near me night's black clouds are rolling,
Gathering o'er a waste of snow.

So I watch the river winding
Through the misty fading plain,
Bitter are the tear-drops blinding,
Bitter useless toil and pain
Bitterest of all the finding
That my dream was false and vain!

A VISION

Gloomy and black are the cypress trees,
Drearily waileth the chill night breeze.
The long grass waveth, the tombs are white,
And the black clouds flit o'er the chill moonlight.
Silent is all save the dropping rain,
When slowly there cometh a mourning train,
The lone churchyard is dark and dim,
And the mourners raise a funeral hymn:

"Open, dark grave, and take her;
Though we have loved her so,
Yet we must now forsake her,
Love will no more awake her:
(Oh, bitter woe!)
Open thine arms and take her
To rest below!

"Vain is our mournful weeping,
Her gentle life is o'er;
Only the worm is creeping,
Where she will soon be sleeping,
For evermore
Nor joy nor love is keeping
For her in store!"

Gloomy and black are the cypress trees,
And drearily wave in the chill night breeze.
The dark clouds part and the heavens are blue,

Where the trembling stars are shining through.
Slowly across the gleaming sky,
A crowd of white angels are passing by.
Like a fleet of swans they float along,
Or the silver notes of a dying song.
Like a cloud of incense their pinions rise,
Fading away up the purple skies.
But hush! for the silent glory is stirred,
By a strain such as earth has never heard:

"Open, oh Heaven! we bear her,
This gentle maiden mild,
Earth's griefs we gladly spare her,
From earthly joys we tear her,
Still undefiled;
And to thine arms we bear her,
Thine own, thy child.

"Open, oh Heaven! no morrow
Will see this joy o'ercast,
No pain, no tears, no sorrow,
Her gentle heart will borrow;
Sad life is past;
Shielded and safe from sorrow,
At home at last."

But the vision faded and all was still,
On the purple valley and distant hill.
No sound was there save the wailing breeze,
The rain, and the rustling cypress trees.

PICTURES IN THE FIRE

What is it you ask me, darling?
All my stories, child, you know;
I have no strange dreams to tell you,
Pictures I have none to show.

Tell you glorious scenes of travel?
Nay, my child, that cannot be,
I have seen no foreign countries,
Marvels none on land or sea.

Yet strange sights in truth I witness,
And I gaze until I tire,
Wondrous pictures, changing ever,
As I look into the fire.

There, last night, I saw a cavern,

Black as pitch; within it lay
Coiled in many folds a dragon,
Glaring as if turned at bay.

And a knight in dismal armour
On a winged eagle came,
To do battle with this dragon;
And his crest was all of flame.

As I gazed the dragon faded,
And, instead, sate Pluto crowned,
By a lake of burning fire;
Spirits dark were crouching round.

That was gone, and lo! before me,
A cathedral vast and grim;
I could almost hear the organ
Peal alone the arches dim.

As I watched the wreathed pillars,
Groves of stately palms arose,
And a group of swarthy Indians
Stealing on some sleeping foes.

Stay; a cataract glancing brightly,
Dashed and sparkled; and beside
Lay a broken marble monster,
Mouth and eyes were staring wide.

Then I saw a maiden wreathing
Starry flowers in garlands sweet;
Did she see the fiery serpent
That was wrapped about her feet?

That fell crashing all and vanished;
And I saw two armies close
I could almost hear the clarions,
And the shouting of the foes.

They were gone; and lo! bright angels,
On a barren mountain wild,
Raised appealing arms to Heaven,
Bearing up a little child.

And I gazed, and gazed, and slowly
Gathered in my eyes sad tears,
And the fiery pictures bore me
Back through distant dreams of years.

Once again I tasted sorrow,
With past joy was once more gay,

Till the shade had gathered round me
And the fire had died away.

Two stranger youths in the Far West,
Beneath the ancient forest trees,
Pausing, amid their toil to rest,
Spake of their home beyond the seas;
Spake of the hearts that beat so warmly,
Of the hearts they loved so well.
In their chilly northern country.
"Would," they cried, "some voice could tell
Where they are, our own beloved ones!"
They looked up to the evening sky
Half hidden by the giant branches,
But heard no angel-voice reply.
All silent was the quiet evening;
Silent were the ancient trees;
They only heard the murmuring song
Of the summer breeze,
That gently played among
The acacia trees.
And did no warning spirit answer,
Amid the silence all around;
"Before the lowly village altar
She thou lovest may be found,
Thou, who trustest still so blindly,
Know she stands a smiling bride!
Forgetting thee, she turneth kindly
To the stranger at her side.
Yes, this day thou art forgotten,
Forgotten, too, thy last farewell,
All the vows that she has spoken,
And thy heart has kept so well.
Dream no more of a starry future,
In thy home beyond the seas!"
But he only heard the gentle sigh
Of the summer breeze,
So softly passing by
The acacia trees.

And vainly, too, the other, looking
Smiling up through hopeful tears,
Asked in his heart of hearts, "Where is she,
She I love these many years?"
He heard no echo calling faintly:
"Lo, she lieth cold and pale,
And her smile so calm and saintly

Heeds not grieving sob or wail
Heeds not the lilies strewn upon her,
Pure as she is, and as white,
Or the solemn chanting voices,
Or the taper's ghastly light."
But silent still was the ancient forest,
Silent were the gloomy trees,
He only heard the wailing sound
Of the summer breeze,
That sadly played around
The acacia trees

HUSH

"I can scarcely hear," she murmured,
"For my heart beats loud and fast,
But surely, in the far, far distance,
I can hear a sound at last."
"It is only the reapers singing,
As they carry home their sheaves,
And the evening breeze has risen,
And rustles the dying leaves."

"Listen! there are voices talking."
Calmly still she strove to speak,
Yet her voice grew faint and trembling,
And the red flushed in her cheek.
"It is only the children playing
Below, now their work is done,
And they laugh that their eyes are dazzled
By the rays of the setting sun."

Fainter grew her voice, and weaker
As with anxious eyes she cried,
"Down the avenue of chestnuts,
I can hear a horseman ride."
"It was only the deer that were feeding
In a herd on the clover grass,
They were startled, and fled to the thicket,
As they saw the reapers pass."

Now the night arose in silence,
Birds lay in their leafy nest,
And the deer couched in the forest,
And the children were at rest:
There was only a sound of weeping
From watchers around a bed,
But Rest to the weary spirit,
Peace to the quiet Dead!

HOURS

When the bright stars came out last night,
And the dew lay on the flowers,
I had a vision of delight
A dream of by-gone hours.

Those hours that came and fled so fast,
Of pleasure or of pain,
As phantoms rose from out the past
Before my eyes again.

With beating heart did I behold
A train of joyous hours,
Lit with the radiant light of old,
And, smiling, crowned with flowers.

And some were hours of childish sorrow,
A mimicry of pain,
That through their tears looked for a morrow
They knew must smile again.

Those hours of hope that longed for life,
And wished their part begun,
And ere the summons to the strife,
Dreamed that the field was won.

I knew the echo of their voice,
The starry crowns they wore;
The vision made my soul rejoice
With the old thrill of yore.

I knew the perfume of their flowers;
The glorious shining rays
Around these happy smiling hours
Were lit in by-gone days.

Oh stay, I cried, bright visions, stay,
And leave me not forlorn!
But, smiling still, they passed away,
Like shadows of the morn.

One spirit still remained, and cried,
"Thy soul shall ne'er forget!"
He standeth ever by my side
The phantom called Regret!

But still the spirits rose, and there

Were weary hours of pain,
And anxious hours of fear and care
Bound by an iron chain.

Dim shadows came of lonely hours,
That shunned the light of day,
And in the opening smile of flowers
Saw only quick decay.

Calm hours that sought the starry skies
For heavenly lore were there;
With folded hands and earnest eyes,
I knew the hours of prayer.

Stern hours that darkened the sun's light,
Heralds of coming woes,
With trailing wings, before my sight
From the dim past arose.

As each dark vision passed and spoke
I prayed it to depart:
At each some buried sorrow woke
And stirred within my heart.

Until these hours of pain and care
Lifted their tearful eyes,
Spread their dark pinions in the air
And passed into the skies.

THE TWO INTERPRETERS

"The clouds are fleeting by, father,
Look in the shining west,
The great white clouds sail onward
Upon the sky's blue breast.
Look at a snowy eagle,
His wings are tinged with red,
And a giant dolphin follows him,
With a crown upon his head!"

The father spake no word, but watched
The drifting clouds roll by;
He traced a misty vision too
Upon the shining sky:
A shadowy form, with well-known grace
Of weary love and care,
Above the smiling child she held,
Shook down her floating hair.

"The clouds are changing now, father,
Mountains rise higher and higher!
And see where red and purple ships
Sail in a sea of fire!"
The father pressed the little hand
More closely in his own,
And watched a cloud-dream in the sky
That he could see alone:
Bright angels carrying far away
A white form, cold and dead,
Two held the feet, and two bore up
The flower-crowned, drooping head.

"See, father, see! a glory floods
The sky, and all is bright,
And clouds of every hue and shade
Burn in the golden light.
And now, above an azure lake,
Rise battlements and towers,
Where knights and ladies climb the heights,
All bearing purple flowers."

The father looked, and, with a pang
Of love and strange alarm,
Drew close the little eager child
Within his sheltering arm;
From out the clouds the mother looks
With wistful glance below,
She seems to seek the treasure left
On earth so long ago;
She holds her arms out to her child,
His cradle-song she sings:
The last rays of the sunset gleam
Upon her outspread wings.

Calm twilight veils the summer sky,
The shining clouds are gone;
In vain the merry laughing child
Still gaily prattles on;
In vain the bright stars, one by one,
On the blue silence start,
A dreary shadow rests to-night
Upon the father's heart

COMFORT

Hast thou o'er the clear heaven of thy soul
Seen tempests roll?
Hast thou watched all the hopes thou wouldst have won

Fade, one by one?
Wait till the clouds are past, then raise thine eyes
To bitter skies.

Hast thou gone sadly through a dreary night,
And found no light,
No guide, no star, to cheer thee through the plain
No friend, save pain?
Wait, and thy soul shall see, when most forlorn,
Rise a new morn.

Hast thou beneath another's stern control
Bent thy sad soul,
And wasted sacred hopes and precious tears?
Yet calm thy fears,
For thou canst gain, even from the bitterest part,
A stronger heart.

Has Fate overwhelmed thee with some sudden blow?
Let thy tears flow;
But know when storms are past, the heavens appear
More pure, more clear;
And hope, when farthest from their shining rays,
For brighter days.

Hast thou found life a cheat, and worn in vain
Its iron chain?
Has thy soul bent beneath earth's heavy bond?
Look thou beyond;
If life is bitter, there forever shine
Hopes more divine.

Art thou alone, and does thy soul complain
It lives in vain?
Not vainly does he live who can endure
Oh be thou sure,
That he who hopes and suffers here, can earn
A sure return.

Hast thou found nought within thy troubled life
Save inward strife?
Hast thou found all she promised thee, Deceit,
And Hope a cheat?
Endure, and there shall dawn within thy breast
Eternal rest!

HOME AT LAST

Child, do not fear;

Still the more his soul must struggle vainly,
Bowed beneath a noble discontent.

No great Thinker ever lived and taught you
All the wonder that his soul received;
No true Painter ever set on canvas
All the glorious vision he conceived.

No Musician ever held your spirit
Charmed and bound in his melodious chains,
But be sure he heard, and strove to render,
Feeble echoes of celestial strains.

No real Poet ever wove in numbers
All his dream; but the diviner part,
Hidden from all the world, spake to him only
In the voiceless silence of his heart.

So with Love: for Love and Art united
Are twin mysteries; different, yet the same:
Poor indeed would be the love of any
Who could find its full and perfect name.

Love may strive, but vain is the endeavour
All its boundless riches to enfold;
Still its tenderest, truest secret lingers
Ever in its deepest depths untold.

Things of Time have voices: speak and perish.
Art and Love speak, but their words must be
Like sighings of illimitable forests,
And waves of an unfathomable sea.

BECAUSE

It is not because your heart is mine, mine only
Mine alone;
It is not because you chose me, weak and lonely,
For your own;
Not because the earth is fairer, and the skies
Spread above you
Are more radiant for the shining of your eyes
That I love you!

It is not because the world's perplexed meaning
Grows more clear;
And the Parapets of Heaven, with angels leaning,
Seem more near;
And Nature sings of praise with all her voices

Since yours spoke,
Since within my silent heart, that now rejoices,
Love awoke!

Nay, not even because your hand holds heart and life;
At your will
Soothing, hushing all its discord, making strife
Calm and still;
Teaching Trust to fold her wings, nor ever roam
From her nest;
Teaching Love that her securest, safest home
Must be Rest.

But because this human Love, though true and sweet
Yours and mine
Has been sent by Love more tender, more complete,
More divine;
That it leads our hearts to rest at last in Heaven,
Far above you;
Do I take you as a gift that God has given
And I love you

REST AT EVENING

When the weariness of Life is ended,
And the task of our long day is done,
And the props, on which our hearts depended,
All have failed or broken, one by one;
Evening and our Sorrow's shadow blended
Telling us that peace is now begun.

How far back will seem the sun's first dawning,
And those early mists so cold and grey!
Half forgotten even the toil of morning,
And the heat and burthen of the day:
Flowers that we were tending, and weeds scorning,
All alike withered and cast away.

Vain will seem the impatient heart, which waited
Toils that gathered but too quickly round;
And the childish joy, so soon elated
At the path we thought none else had found;
And the foolish ardour, soon abated
By the storm which cast us to the ground.

Vain those pauses on the road, each seeming
As our final home and resting-place;
And the leaving them, while tears were streaming
Of eternal sorrow down our face;

And the hands we held, fond folly dreaming
That no future could their touch efface.

All will then be faded:—night will borrow
Stars of light to crown our perfect rest;
And the dim vague memory of faint sorrow
Just remain to show us all was best,
Then melt into a divine to-morrow:—
Oh, how poor a day to be so blest!

A RETROSPECT

From this fair point of present bliss,
Where we together stand,
Let me look back once more, and trace
That long and desert land,
Wherein till now was cast my lot, and I could live, and thou wert not.

Strange that my heart could beat, and know
Alternate joy and pain,
That suns could roll from east to west,
And clouds could pass in rain,
And the slow hours without thee fleet, nor stay their noiseless silver feet.

What had I then? a hope, that grew
Each hour more bright and dear,
The flush upon the eastern skies
That showed the sun was near:—
Now night has faded far away, my sun has risen, and it is day.

A dim Ideal of tender grace
In my soul reigned supreme;
Too noble and too sweet I thought
To live, save in a dream
Within thy heart to-day it lies, and looks on me from thy dear eyes.

Some gentle spirit, Love I thought
Built many a shrine of pain;
Though each false Idol fell to dust,
The worship was not vain,
But a faint radiant shadow cast back from our Love upon the Past.

And Grief, too, held her vigil there;
With unrelenting sway
Breaking my cloudy visions down,
Throwing my flowers away:—
I owe to her fond care alone that I may now be all thine own.

Fair Joy was there, her fluttering wings

At times she strove to raise;
Watching through long and patient nights,
Listening long eager days:
I know now that her heart and mine were waiting, Love, to welcome thine.

Thus I can read thy name throughout,
And, now her task is done,
Can see that even that faded Past
Was thine, beloved one,
And so rejoice my Life may be all consecrated, dear, to thee.

TRUE OR FALSE

So you think you love me, do you?
Well, it may be so;
But there are many ways of loving
I have learnt to know.
Many ways, and but one true way,
Which is very rare;
And the counterfeits look brightest,
Though they will not wear.

Yet they ring, almost, quite truly,
Last (with care) for long;
But in time must break, may shiver
At a touch of wrong:
Having seen what looked most real
Crumble into dust;
Now I chose that test and trial
Should precede my trust.

I have seen a love demanding
Time and hope and tears,
Chaining all the past, exacting
Bonds from future years;
Mind and heart, and joy and sorrow,
Claiming as its fee:
That was Love of Self, and never,
Never Love of me!

I have seen a love forgetting
All above, beyond,
Linking every dream and fancy
In a sweeter bond;
Counting every hour worthless,
Which was cold or free:—
That, perhaps, was, Love of Pleasure,
But not Love of me!

I have seen a love whose patience
Never turned aside,
Full of tender, fond devices;
Constant, even when tried;
Smallest boons were held as victories,
Drops that swelled the sea:
That I think was, Love of Power,
But not Love of me!

I have seen a love disdaining
Ease and pride and fame,
Burning even its own white pinions
Just to feed its flame;
Reigning thus, supreme, triumphant,
By the soul's decree;
That was Love of Love, I fancy,
But not Love of me!

I have heard or dreamt, it may be
What Love is when true;
How to test and how to try it,
Is the gift of few:
These few say (or did I dream it?)
That true Love abides
In these very things, but always
Has a soul besides.

Lives among the false loves, knowing
Just their peace and strife:
Bears the self-same look, but always
Has an inner life.
Only a true heart can find it,
True as it is true,
Only eyes as clear and tender
Look it through and through.

If it dies, it will not perish
By Time's slow decay,
True Love only grows (they tell me)
Stronger, day by day:
Pain, has been its friend and comrade;
Fate, it can defy;
Only by its own sword, sometimes
Love can choose to die.

And its grave shall be more noble
And more sacred still,
Than a throne, where one less worthy
Reigns and rules at will.
Tell me then, do you dare offer
This true Love to me? . . .

Neither you nor I can answer;
We will wait and see!

GOLDEN WORDS

Some words are played on golden strings,
Which I so highly rate,
I cannot bear for meaner things
Their sound to desecrate.

For every day they are not meet,
Or for a careless tone;
They are for rarest, and most sweet,
And noblest use alone.

One word is POET: which is flung
So carelessly away,
When such as you and I have sung,
We hear it, day by day.

Men pay it for a tender phrase
Set in a cadenced rhyme:
I keep it as a crown of praise
To crown the kings of time.

And LOVE: the slightest feelings, stirred
By trivial fancy, seek
Expression in that golden word
They tarnish while they speak.

Nay, let the heart's slow, rare decree,
That word in reverence keep
Silence herself should only be
More sacred and more deep.

FOR EVER: men have grown at length
To use that word, to raise
Some feeble protest into strength,
Or turn some tender phrase.

It should be said in awe and fear
By true heart and strong will,
And burn more brightly year by year,
A starry witness still.

HONOUR: all trifling hearts are fond
Of that divine appeal,
And men, upon the slightest bond,
Set it as slighter seal.

That word should meet a noble foe
Upon a noble field,
And echo like a deadly blow
Turned by a silver shield.

Trust me, the worth of words is such
They guard all noble things,
And that this rash irreverent touch
Has jarred some golden strings.

For what the lips have lightly said
The heart will lightly hold,
And things on which we daily tread
Are lightly bought and sold.

The sun of every day will bleach
The costliest purple hue.
And so our common daily speech
Discolours what was true.

But as you keep some thoughts apart
In sacred honoured care,
If in the silence of your heart,
Their utterance too be rare;

Then, while a thousand words repeat
Unmeaning clamours all,
Melodious golden echoes sweet
Shall answer when you call.

Adelaide Anne Proctor – A Short Biography

Adelaide Anne Procter was born on 30th October, 1825 at 25 Bedford Square in the Bloomsbury district of London, to the poet Bryan Waller Procter and his wife Anne (née Skepper).

Procter's literary career began early, whilst still a teenager. Many of her poems were published by the great Charles Dickens in his periodicals Household Words and All the Year Round before being later published in book form.

Indeed, Dickens was formative in her career and spoke highly of her intelligence. She seemed to be able to fully focus and master without difficulty any subject she wished.

As a young child, she became familiar with several of the problems of Euclid. As she grew she added French, Italian, and German as well as piano-forte and drawing to her array of talents. But, it seems that as soon as a subject was mastered her interest passed and she was on to another.

A voracious reader, Procter was largely self-taught, though she did study at Queen's College in Harley Street in 1850. Her interest in poetry grew from an early age. Accounts say that she carried with her a tiny album into which her favourite passages were copied for her by her mother before she herself could write. Preferring poetry to dolls and the like was certainly an indication of her future career path.

Procter published her first poem, Ministering Angels, while still a teenager. The poem appeared in Heath's Book of Beauty in 1843.

By 1853 she was submitting pieces to Dickens's Household Words under her pseudonym Mary Berwick, electing that this way her work would be judged for its own worth rather than on the friendship between her father and Dickens. Dickens didn't learn of her true identity for over a year.

Minstering Angels was to be the beginning of a long and mutually beneficial relationship of publishing in Dickens' journals that would eventually reach 73 poems in House words together with a further 7 poems in All the Year Round, most of which were collected and later published into her first two volumes of poetry, both entitled Legends and Lyrics. Her work was also published in Good Words and Cornhill.

Proctor was also the editor of the journal Victoria Regia, which became the showpiece of the Victoria Press, a venture hoping to promote the employment of women in all manner of trades and professions.

In 1851, Procter had converted to Roman Catholicism and become extremely active in several charitable and feminist causes. She was a member of the Langham Place Group, which set out to improve conditions for women, and was friends with many feminists including Bessie Rayner Parkes and Barbara Leigh Smith. Procter helped found the English Woman's Journal in 1858 and, in 1859, the Society for the Promotion of the Employment of Women, both of which focused on expanding women's economic and employment opportunities. Though on paper Proctor was merely one member among many, fellow-member Jessie Boucherett considered her to be the "animating spirit" of the Society. Her third volume of poetry, A Chaplet of Verses (1861), was published for the benefit of a Catholic Night Refuge for Women and Children that had been founded in 1860 at Providence Row in East London.

Her personal life remains a little unclear. Accounts suggest that in 1858 Procter became engaged, although to whom remains unknown and the marriage never took place.

Other accounts suggest the engagement lasted several years before being broken off by her fiancé. Another goes so far as to suggest that she was a lesbian and in love with Matilda Hays, a fellow member of the Society for the Promotion of the Employment of Women; other critics have called Procter's relationship with Hays "emotionally intense." Procter's first volume of poetry, Legends and Lyrics (1858) was dedicated to Hays and that same year Procter wrote a poem titled "To M.M.H." in which Procter "expresses love for Hays. Matilda Hays herself was a novelist and translator of George Sand and a somewhat controversial figure. She liked to dress in men's clothes and had lived with the sculptor Harriet Hosmer in Rome earlier in the 1850s." The true extent of her relationship cannot be verified and it should always be seen in proportion to her Catholicism.

Procter's health failed in 1862. Dickens and others suggested that this illness was due to her extensive and exhausting schedule of charity work.

An attempt to improve her health by taking a cure at Malvern failed.

We shall reach our home to-night,
For the sky is clear,
And the waters bright;
And the breezes have scarcely strength
To unfold that little cloud,
That like a shroud
Spreads out its fleecy length
Then have no fear,
As we cleave our silver way
Through the waters clear.

Fear not, my child!
Though the waves are white and high,
And the storm blows wild
Through the gloomy sky;
On the edge of the western sea,
See that line of golden light,
Is the haven bright
Where home is awaiting thee;
Where, this peril past,
We shall rest from our stormy voyage
In peace at last.

Be not afraid;
But give me thy hand, and see
How the waves have made
A cradle for thee.
Night is come, dear, and we shall rest;
So turn from the angry skies,
And close thine eyes,
And lay thy head on my breast:
Child, do not weep;
In the calm, cold, purple depths
There we shall sleep.

UNEXPRESSED

Dwells within the soul of every Artist
More than all his effort can express;
And he knows the best remains unuttered;
Sighing at what we call his success.

Vainly he may strive; he dare not tell us
All the sacred mysteries of the skies:
Vainly he may strive; the deepest beauty
Cannot be unveiled to mortal eyes.

And the more devoutly that he listens,
And the holier message that is sent,

Adelaide Anne Proctor died on 3rd February 1864 of tuberculosis. She had been bed-ridden for almost a year. Procter was buried in Kensal Green Cemetery.

Her death was described in the press as a "national calamity". Indeed, Procter was the favourite poet of Queen Victoria. The Victorian poet Coventry Patmore, himself a highly respected poet of the time, called her the most popular poet of the day, after Alfred, Lord Tennyson. Procter's popularity continued after her death; the first volume of Legends and Lyrics went through 19 editions by 1881, and the second volume through 14 editions by the same year.

Many of her poems were made into hymns or otherwise set to music. Among these was "The Lost Chord", which Arthur Sullivan set to music in 1877, was the most commercially successful of the 1870s and 1880s in both Britain and the United States.

However, by the turn of the century her work had fallen from fashion and has never recovered.

Procter's poetry was strongly influenced by her religious beliefs, charity work and her desire for social reform. Homelessness, poverty, and fallen women are frequent themes in her verse.

Adelaide Anne Proctor – A Concise Bibliography

'Three Evenings in the House,' a short story written for A House to Let (1858), one of the collaborative Christmas numbers of the Charles Dickens' journal Household Words.

Legends and Lyrics. First series (1858)

'The Ghost in the Picture Room' written for A Haunted House (1859)

Legends and Lyrics. Second series (1861)

A Chaplet of Verses (1862)